A2 Music Listening Tests

Book 1

Edexcel

Hugh Benham and Alistair Wightman

R.

Rhinegold Education
239–241 Shaftesbury Avenue
London WC2H 8TF
Telephone: 020 7333 1720
Fax: 020 7333 1765

www.rhinegold.co.uk

Rhinegold Music Study Guides
(series editor: Paul Terry)

For Edexcel Specifications:
GCSE Music Study Guide
GCSE Music Listening Tests (Books 1, 2, 3 and 4)
AS Music Study Guide
AS Music Listening Tests for Students (Books 1 and 2)
A2 Music Study Guide
A2 Music Listening Tests (Books 1 and 2)
AS/A2 Music Technology Study Guide
Listening Tests for Students: Edexcel Music Technology AS and A2 Music Specification

Similar books have been produced for the AQA and OCR Music Specifications. Also available are:
GCSE Music Study Guide for the WJEC Specification (separate English- and Welsh-language versions)

Other Rhinegold Study Guides
AS and A2 Drama and Theatre Studies Study Guides (AQA and Edexcel)
AS and A2 Performance Studies Study Guides (OCR)
AS and A2 Religious Studies Study Guides (AQA, Edexcel and OCR)

Rhinegold Publishing also publishes Classical Music, Classroom Music, Early Music Today, Music Teacher, Opera Now, Piano, Teaching Drama, The Singer, British and International Music Yearbook, British Performing Arts Yearbook, Rhinegold Dictionary of Music in Sound, British Music Education Yearbook.

First published 2004 in Great Britain by
Rhinegold Publishing Ltd
241 Shaftesbury Avenue
London WC2H 8TF
Telephone: 020 7333 1720
Fax: 020 7333 1765
www.rhinegold.co.uk

© Rhinegold Publishing Ltd 2004
Reprinted 2005, 2006, 2008

All rights reserved. No part of this publication may be reproduced, stored in a retrieval system, or transmitted in any form or by any means, electronic, mechanical, photocopying, recording or otherwise, without the prior permission of Rhinegold Publishing Ltd.

Unauthorised copying of this material is illegal.

Rhinegold Publishing Ltd has used its best efforts in preparing this guide. It does not assume, and hereby disclaims, any liability to any party for loss or damage caused by errors or omissions in the guide whether such errors or omissions result from negligence, accident or other cause.

You should always check the current requirements of the examination, since these may change. Copies of the Edexcel specification may be obtained from Edexcel Examinations at Edexcel Publications, Adamsway, Mansfield, Notts., NG18 4FN
Telephone 01623 467467, Facsimile 01623 450481, Email publications@linneydirect.com
See also the Edexcel website at www.edexcel.org.uk

A2 Music Listening Tests Book 1: Edexcel
British Library Cataloguing in Publication Data.
A catalogue record for this book is available from the British Library.

ISBN 978-1-906178-56-7

Printed in Great Britain by Headley Brothers Ltd

The authors

Hugh Benham has been involved in the examining of A level and GCE Music since 1981. For 20 years he was head of the music department in a large sixth-form college, and he has considerable experience in adult education and INSET. He is a church organist, has contributed to *The New Grove Dictionary of Music and Musicians* (2001), and is the author of two books on English church music, one of which, *John Taverner: His Life and Music*, was published by Ashgate in 2003. He has contributed to *Music Teacher* magazine, has written articles on early music, and was the editor of Taverner's complete works for *Early English Church Music* (published by Stainer and Bell for The British Academy).

Alistair Wightman has worked in primary, secondary and further education, and continues to teach at the Staffordshire County Council School for Talented Young Musicians. He is also a freelance teacher and writer, and serves as a principal examiner in music history and analysis in A-level music with one of the English examination boards. In addition to appearing as a pianist, both as a soloist and as a member of the Chiarina Trio, he pursues an interest in Polish music, his publications including several books and articles devoted to Tadeusz Baird, Karlowicz and Szymanowski.

Acknowledgments

The authors would particularly like to thank Jamie Masters of Audiolab for his invaluable role in producing the CD. Ann Farmer, Emma Findlow, Joanna Hughes, Lucien Jenkins, Peter Nickol, Elisabeth Rhodes, Katherine Smith, Paul Terry and Abigail Walmsley have all been generous in their expert support during the preparation of this guide.

Nevertheless if any errors have been made it is only right to state that these are the responsibility of the authors.

Compact disc

A CD containing recordings of all the extracts for the listening tests in this book is available from Rhinegold Book Sales, 241 Shaftesbury Avenue, London, WC2H 8TF, tel. +44 (0)20 7333 1720, fax. +44 (0)20 7333 1765, email sales@rhinegold.co.uk or order online at www.rhinegold.co.uk.

Recordings

The authors are grateful to Naxos and BMG UK and Ireland Limited who have granted permission for the use of their recordings.

Introduction

If you've already worked through the companion book on AS Listening, you may remember that we stressed there the need for **lots of practice**. A2 Listening requires as much – or preferably even more.

What this book is for This book is to help you do as well as you possibly can in the Edexcel GCE A2 Listening Paper (Paper 61) by providing you with a range of practice materials with answers.

How to use this book The book has examples of each type of question you will encounter in the exam. You answer these by listening to the accompanying CD.

You can use the tests to gain experience in coping with the stresses and strains of the exam situation, but you might also work through them in a more relaxed way to improve your knowledge, skills and understanding. You'll probably find it useful to work some of the tests a second time once you've had a chance to forget the answers.

In the exam, because you will have your own CD, you can choose the number of times you hear each excerpt of music within the overall time of one hour. You'll have to ration yourself quite strictly, however, especially with the less demanding questions. But in the early stages of preparation, don't feel guilty about listening over and over until you get the point.

Answers to all the questions are given at the back of this book. You will probably find it most useful to consult these answers after trying the questions on your own. In a few cases we have provided hints in the main part of the book, to give you a helping hand.

The types of questions For A2 Music you have to do three questions. For the first two, there is no printed music: you just listen and draw on your musical experience. For the third, you will also have an outline or 'skeleton' score.

1. **Context:** You hear three excerpts, and will be asked to say what type of music each is, and to suggest dates of composition and composers.

2. **Comparisons:** You have to describe similarities and differences between two excerpts.

3. **General Test of Aural Perception:** You have to answer various questions that include the filling in of rhythms or pitches that are missing in the score, identification of chords and keys, writing about the music you hear and its social and historical background.

More detail on each task follows in the appropriate chapter. But you **must also read** the full requirements as set out in the specification (or syllabus) for Edexcel GCE Music. Your teacher will have a copy, but this information can be accessed on the Edexcel website as well (www.edexcel.org.uk). **Remember that specifications can change from time to time**, and it is your teacher's responsibility and yours to know about any such changes.

How to do as well as you possibly can in the exam

1. **In preparation for the exam** make sure you know how to operate the CD player that you will be using in the exam. If the machine is battery-operated, make sure you have spare batteries.

2. **Read the question.** You might even try to predict one or two answers – but...

3. **Always write down what you actually hear rather than what you expect to hear.**

4. **Don't panic.** The best advice of all! Even if listening exams are not

your favourite thing, remember that each year's paper is designed to have some easy bits to give you confidence. Not panicking will help you to…

5. **Concentrate.** With a limited amount of time you can't afford to 'switch off' or day-dream.

6. **You've got to manage that hour really effectively.** You will have your own recording, and you can hear each track as many times as you like, but as the question paper warns you, listening to some tracks too frequently may mean that you don't have time to listen enough to the others.

    The exam CD will contain six excerpts, three for Question 1, two for Question 2, and a single longer one for Question 3. Each piece will occupy a single track, except for Question 3, which will be divided up into several tracks. The reason for this is explained on page 22.

7. **Look at the number of marks for each question.** As Question 3 carries about half the marks for the paper, allow not less than half the time for it. Some people would advise you to start with this question. We would suggest that you begin with Question 1, which is more straightforward, and, if it goes well, will boost your confidence.

8. **Do make sufficient points** on the larger questions. If you see that a question is worth four marks, you'll need to make four valid points. But remember…

9. **Lots of words do not always equal lots of marks.** Make sure that what you write is relevant. But if you can't think of the right technical words in the heat of moment, don't be afraid to use a phrase or sentence to explain what you mean.

How to prepare

1. **Lots of practice** as indicated above.

2. **Learn how to listen.** Much of modern life is visually orientated, and although we **hear** what's going on, we're not used to **listening** intently. Breaking out of this non-listening mode is important if you're to do well in aural exams.

3. **Learn the technical words.** Yes, you can answer with long-winded phrases or sentences rather than precise technical terms. But, you must know these technical words because at least some of them are used in the questions you'll have to answer.

    If you come across technical words in this book that you don't understand, look in the glossary of the *AS Music Study Guide* for the Edexcel Specification (Rhinegold Publishing 2008). An excellent source of reference when preparing for a listening paper is the *Rhinegold Dictionary of Music in Sound* (Rhinegold Publishing 2002).

4. **Learn from other parts of your course.** For example, if for Paper 51 you're working on the Chorale or the 32-bar Pop Song, you will have many opportunities for listening to different types of chords.

Question 1: Context

Introduction

For Question 1 of the A2 Listening Paper (Paper 61), you will hear three excerpts. In each case you will be asked to identify the type of music, to suggest a date of composition, and a composer. With popular music, you may instead have to name a performer or a band. You may need to give reasons for your choices. No musical notation will be given.

How can you learn to do well in the Context question? Answer: by comparing the music you hear in the exam with music you've already heard and whose identity you know. So the more music you listen to the better. Listen carefully to the whole of *The New Anthology of Music* – not just the Areas of Study you do for Papers 32 and 62; in doing this you will hear something in most styles that the examiners are likely to choose from. Each Area of Study is arranged in chronological order so this will help you appreciate how music has changed over time.

Don't spend too long on the Context questions. Generally speaking, you'll either know the answers more or less straight away or you won't. Try limiting yourself to two hearings of each excerpt, and see how you get on. If you don't know the answers, look on this positively: there's more learning to be done!

After you've worked the following tests it is easy to find your own practice material. Switch on the radio and identify what you hear, or get friends to test you on pieces they are learning to play or with randomly selected tracks from CDs.

The following 24 excerpts are grouped in threes to provide you with eight complete specimen questions.

Test 1 **Tracks 1–3**

Answer all THREE parts of this question.

(a) **The music for Excerpt A is on Track 1.**

  (i) From what type of piece is this excerpt taken? Underline your answer.

   air   lied   recitative   verse anthem (1)

  (ii) Suggest a possible year of composition. (2)

   ....

   Advice: Suggest a **single** year of composition (e.g. 1590 or 1950) rather than a time period such as 1720–50. You're not expected to know the precise year, but mark schemes typically reward 'Any (single) year from x to y'. Likewise, give the name of just one composer.

  (iii) Name a possible composer of this excerpt.

   ....

   (1)

(b) **The music for Excerpt B is on Track 2.**

  (i) From what type of work is this excerpt taken?

   ....

   (1)

  (ii) Suggest a possible year of composition.

   ....

   (2)

  (iii) Name a possible composer of this excerpt.

   ....

   (1)

(c) **The music for Excerpt C is on Track 3.**

  (i) Identify the style of music as precisely as you can.

   ....

   (2)

  (ii) In which of the following time spans was the music composed? Underline your answer.

   1920–30   1940–50   1960–70   1980–90   (1)

  (iii) Name a possible composer of this excerpt.

   ....

   (1)

   (Total 12 marks)

8 Question 1: Context

Test 2 Tracks 4–6

Answer all THREE parts of this question.

(a) **The music for Excerpt A is on Track 4.**

   (i) You will hear the ending of one piece and the beginning of another, both from the same extended work. What type of piece is each?

   First piece .... **(1)**

   Second piece .... **(1)**

   (ii) Suggest a possible year of composition.

   .... **(1)**

   (iii) Name a possible composer of this excerpt.

   .... **(1)**

(b) **The music for Excerpt B is on Track 5.**

   (i) Which of the following best describes the musical style of the excerpt? Underline your answer.

   expressionism   impressionism   minimalism

   neo-classicism   serialism **(1)**

   Advice: If, when answering this question, you did not know the meaning of one or more of the terms given above, refer to *The Rhinegold Dictionary of Music in Sound* so that you will know next time!

   (ii) Suggest a possible year of composition.

   .... **(2)**

   (iii) Name a possible composer of this excerpt.

   .... **(1)**

(c) **The music for Excerpt C is on Track 6.**

   (i) Identify the style of music as precisely as you can.

   .... **(2)**

   (ii) From which decade of the 20th century (e.g. 1990s) does this music come?

   .... **(1)**

   (iii) Give the name of EITHER the trumpet player OR the alto sax player.

   .... **(1)**

(Total 12 marks)

Test 3   **Tracks 7–9**

Answer all THREE parts of this question.

(a) **The music for Excerpt A is on Track 7.**

    (i) From what type of work is this excerpt taken?

        .... (1)

    (ii) Suggest a possible year of composition.

        .... (2)

    (iii) Name a possible composer of this excerpt.

        .... (1)

(b) **The music for Excerpt B is on Track 8.**

    (i) From what type of work is this excerpt taken?

        .... (1)

    (ii) In which of the following time-spans was the music composed? Underline your answer.

        1810–30   1850–70   1890–1910   1930–50   (1)

    (iii) Name a possible composer of this excerpt.

        .... (2)

(c) **The music for Excerpt C is on Track 9.**

    (i) Which of the following musical styles is heard in this excerpt? Underline your answer.

        blues   gospel   ragtime   soul   (1)

    (ii) In which decade of the 20th century (e.g. 1990s) was this recording made?

        .... (2)

    (iii) Which of the following singers do you hear? Underline your answer.

        Billie Holiday   Bessie Smith   Marlene Dietrich   Ella Fitzgerald   (1)

(Total 12 marks)

Question 1: Context

Test 4 Tracks 10–12

Answer all THREE parts of this question.

(a) The music for Excerpt A is on Track 10.

  (i) For what purpose was this music composed?

  .... (1)

  (ii) Suggest a possible year of composition.

  .... (2)

  (iii) Name a possible composer of this excerpt.

  .... (1)

(b) The music for Excerpt B is on Track 11.

  (i) In what circumstances was this music originally performed?

  .... (1)

  (ii) In which **one** of the following years was the music composed? Underline your answer.

             1801   1851   1901   1951 (1)

  (iii) Who composed it? Underline your answer.

      Beethoven   Chopin   Liszt   Ravel   Shostakovich (2)

> **Advice:** You will get credit for a correct answer to (ii) even if your answer to (iii) contradicts this (e.g. Beethoven was not alive in 1951). But try gradually to build an historical perspective by clearly linking names and dates.

(c) The music for Excerpt C is on Track 12.

  (i) In what circumstances did this performance take place?

  .... (2)

  (ii) Which of the following best describes the musical style of the excerpt? Underline your answer.

      grunge   hard rock   pop   soft rock   soul (1)

  (iii) Suggest a year in which this music might have first been performed.

  .... (1)

(Total 12 marks)

Question 1: Context 11

Test 5 Tracks 13–15

Answer all THREE parts of this question.

(a) **The music for Excerpt A is on Track 13.**

  (i) Suggest a possible year of composition.

  .... (1)

  (ii) Give **two** reasons to support your answer.

  ....

  .... (2)

  (iii) Which one of the following composers wrote this music? Underline your answer.

  Palestrina   Byrd   Corelli   Purcell   Handel (1)

(b) **The music for Excerpt B is on Track 14.**

  (i) Identify the style of music.

  .... (1)

  (ii) Suggest a possible year for the first release of this recording.

  .... (2)

  (iii) Name the singer.

  .... (1)

(c) **The music for Excerpt C is on Track 15.**

  (i) Which of the following words best describes the style of this music? Underline your answer.

  romantic   post-romantic   impressionist   expressionist   neo-classical (1)

  (ii) Suggest a possible year of composition.

  .... (2)

  (iii) Name a possible composer of this excerpt.

  .... (1)

(Total 12 marks)

Question 1: Context

Test 6 Tracks 16–18

Answer all THREE parts of this question.

(a) **The music for Excerpt A is on Track 16.**

   (i) Name the type of monophonic music that you hear in the first part of the excerpt.

   .... (1)

   (ii) Which of the following terms or expressions describes the second part of the excerpt? Underline your answer.

   anthem   madrigal   sacred polyphony   secular polyphony   (1)

   (iii) Suggest a possible year of composition for the second part of the excerpt.

   .... (2)

(b) **The music for Excerpt B is on Track 17.**

   (i) Of which musical style is this an example? Underline your answer.

   expressionism   impressionism   minimalism

   nationalism   neo-classicism   (1)

   (ii) Suggest a possible year of composition.

   .... (2)

   (iii) Name a possible composer of this excerpt.

   .... (1)

(c) **The music for Excerpt C is on Track 18.**

   (i) Identify the style of music as precisely as you can.

   .... (2)

   (ii) In which decade of the 20th century might this music have first been performed? Underline your answer.

   1920s   1940s   1960s   1980s   (1)

   (iii) Name a possible bandleader.

   .... (1)

(Total 12 marks)

Question 1: Context   13

Test 7   Tracks 19–21

Answer all THREE parts of this question.

(a) **The music for Excerpt A is on Track 19.**

   (i)   From what type of work is this excerpt taken? Underline your answer.

         concert march   concert waltz   folk-song suite

                symphonic scherzo   theme and variations   (1)

   > **Advice:** You may need to employ a process of elimination. If, for example, the music is in quadruple time, it is not a waltz, if in triple time, it cannot be a march, etc.

   (ii) Suggest a possible year of composition.

         ....   (2)

   (iii) Which one of the following composers wrote this music? Underline your answer.

         Elgar   Fauré   Richard Strauss   Vaughan Williams   Wagner   (1)

(b) **The music for Excerpt B is on Track 20.**

   (i)   Identify the style of music.

         ....   (1)

   (ii) Suggest a possible year of composition.

         ....   (2)

   (iii) Name a possible composer of this excerpt.

         ....   (1)

(c) **The music for Excerpt C is on Track 21.**

   (i)   Identify the style of music.

         ....   (1)

   (ii) Suggest a possible year of composition.

         ....   (2)

   (iii) Which of the following singers do you hear? Underline your answer.

         Elton John   Tom Jones   Elvis Presley   Neil Sedaka   Frank Sinatra   (1)

                                                                                   (Total 12 marks)

14 Question 1: Context

Test 8 Tracks 22–24

Answer all THREE parts of this question.

(a) **The music for Excerpt A is on Track 22.**

   (i) What type of piece is this?

      .... (2)

   (ii) Of which time span is this music typical? Underline your answer.

      1650–90   1710–50   1770–1810   1830–70 (1)

   (iii) Name a possible composer of this excerpt.

      .... (1)

(b) **The music for Excerpt B is on Track 23.**

   (i) From which one of the following types of work is this excerpt most likely to have come? Underline your answer.

      concerto grosso   flute concerto

      octet for strings and wind

      sonata   symphony (1)

   (ii) Suggest a possible year of composition.

      .... (2)

   (iii) Name a possible composer of this excerpt.

      .... (1)

(c) **The music for Excerpt C is on Track 24.**

   (i) Identify the style of music as precisely as you can.

      .... (2)

   (ii) Suggest a possible year of composition.

      .... (1)

   (iii) Which one of the following composed, and performed in, the excerpt? Underline your answer.

      Duke Ellington   Glenn Miller   Thelonious Monk

      Charlie Parker   Bessie Smith (1)

(Total 12 marks)

Question 2: Comparisons

Introduction

➤ Unlike Performance A and Performance B of an AS Comparisons question, the excerpts you hear for A2 will not be substantially the same, and you will be required to listen out for both similarities and differences. Some excerpts are a little longer than is usual in 'real' exams. This should give you additional scope for practice and experience of time-management.

➤ Yes, you will be in charge of time-management. You will need to impose a limit on the number of hearings you allow yourself. Whenever possible, try to distinguish between those questions which might be answered at a general level (perhaps the true/false questions about the presence of certain instruments, major/minor contrasts and so on), and those that will require more detailed investigation.

➤ Differences may involve change of key. If you can state the relationship (e.g. dominant, relative major or minor, or perhaps tertiary), so much the better. Aim to do this, even if you are blessed with perfect pitch. It will help you develop a better understanding of how tonality works.

➤ When asked about similarities, don't hesitate to state the obvious (e.g. the same key, the same melody, the same instrument or family of instruments, the same playing technique). Some very obvious comparisons (such as 'same composer' where this is stated in the question) will not be awarded any marks but neither will they cause you to lose marks.

➤ Look at the number of marks available for each question as this will give you an idea of the quantity of information required. If the question is worth six marks, aim to make at least six separate points in your answer. Don't hesitate to add more points if you think they are relevant but avoid repeating yourself, or reiterating anything which has appeared in previous questions, even if you have expressed yourself in a different way. You won't gain marks for repetition, however eloquent. Refer to pages 22–23 for further information on the sort of points the examiners hope you are going to make.

➤ In questions that refer to just one extract (e.g. 'Only Excerpt A includes strings: TRUE or FALSE?') make sure that you note in rough what occurs in BOTH extracts. For example, you might decide 'There are strings in A' and 'There are strings in B'. This will make it much easier to deduce that, in this case, the answer is FALSE.

➤ You may be required to give a date and composer's name. Try to develop your awareness of musical styles through the ages by extensive listening.

➤ Try to enjoy the music.

16 Question 2: Comparisons

Test 1 **Tracks 25 & 26**

The following questions require you to compare and contrast TWO excerpts of music. The music for Excerpt A is on Track 25. The music for Excerpt B is on Track 26.

Excerpt A is taken from the beginning of a large-scale orchestral work. Excerpt B is the ending of the same work.

> **Note:** In answering parts (a), (b) and (c) concentrate on the early part of each excerpt (about the first 40 seconds).

(a) Underline the word TRUE or FALSE as appropriate below.

　(i)　Excerpt A begins more quietly than Excerpt B.　　　　　　　　TRUE　　FALSE　　(1)

　(ii)　Off-beat accents occur in Excerpt B.　　　　　　　　　　　　TRUE　　FALSE　　(1)

　(iii)　Both excerpts are in triple time.　　　　　　　　　　　　　　TRUE　　FALSE　　(1)

　(iv)　Both excerpts begin in a major key.　　　　　　　　　　　　　TRUE　　FALSE　　(1)

(b) Each excerpt begins with an introduction before the presentation of an important theme. Give **three** differences between these two introductions. You may, for example, consider which introduction is the longer, and point out differences of orchestration.

　..

　..

　.. **(3)**

(c) Compare and contrast the first few bars from the passage that follows the introduction in Excerpt A with the corresponding passage in Excerpt B.

　..

　..

　..

　.. **(4)**

(d) Identify **three** important differences between the excerpts in their later stages. You may, for example, refer to instrumentation, melody, rhythm and tempo.

　..

　..

　.. **(3)**

(e) (i)　To which of the following time spans do the excerpts belong? Underline your answer.

　　　　　1810–30　　　　1850–70　　　　1890–1910　　　　1930–50　　　　　　(1)

　(ii)　Which one of the following composers wrote these excerpts? Underline your answer.

　　　　　Beethoven　　　Britten　　　Elgar　　　Stravinsky　　　Vaughan Williams　　(1)

(Total 16 marks)

Test 2 **Tracks 27 & 28**

Question 2: Comparisons

The following questions require you to compare and contrast TWO excerpts of music. The music for Excerpt A is on Track 27. The music for Excerpt B is on Track 28.

The excerpts are taken from different sections of the same orchestral movement.

(a) Underline the word TRUE or FALSE as appropriate below.

    (i) Both excerpts begin at a quick tempo.   TRUE   FALSE   **(1)**

    (ii) Only the opening of Excerpt B involves strings and woodwind.   TRUE   FALSE   **(1)**

    (iii) At the beginning, only Excerpt A has a descending scalic passage.   TRUE   FALSE   **(1)**

    (iv) Both excerpts begin in compound time.   TRUE   FALSE   **(1)**

(b) Mention **three** other ways in which the introductions of the two excerpts are either similar or different. Do not repeat points covered in question (a).

    ....

    ....

    .... **(3)**

(c) After their introductions have finished, are both excerpts based on the same main theme? Underline the correct answer below.

                  YES   NO   **(1)**

(d) Identify any significant **differences** in the later parts of these excerpts. Refer, for example, to instrumentation, tonality and tempo.

    ....

    ....

    ....

    ....

    ....

    .... **(6)**

(e) (i) In which of the following years were both excerpts composed? Underline your answer.

        1839   1879   1919   1959   **(1)**

    (ii) Which one of the following composers wrote these excerpts? Underline your answer.

         Berlioz   Grieg   Richard Strauss   Sibelius   Wagner   **(1)**

(Total 16 marks)

18 Question 2: Comparisons

Test 3 Tracks 29 & 30

The following questions require you to compare and contrast TWO excerpts of music. The music for Excerpt A is on Track 29. The music for Excerpt B is on Track 30.

Both excerpts are taken from the same movement.

(a) Underline the word TRUE or FALSE as appropriate below.

  (i)   Both excerpts are in quadruple metre.   TRUE   FALSE   (1)

  (ii) Timpani play a more prominent role in Excerpt A.   TRUE   FALSE   (1)

  (iii) There is a passage in octaves at the end of Excerpt A only. TRUE   FALSE   (1)

  (iv) A chromatic scale occurs in Excerpt B only.   TRUE   FALSE   (1)

(b) Compare and contrast the first statements of the opening theme in each excerpt (i.e. about the first 20 seconds).

  ....

  ....

  .... (3)

(c) Comment on any **differences** between the excerpts. You may, for example, refer to instrumentation, tonality and texture.

  ....

  ....

  ....

  ....

  .... (5)

(d) From what type of work do you think both excerpts come? Underline your answer.

  concerto   sonata   symphony   variations   (1)

(e) (i) Suggest a year of composition for these excerpts.

  ....   (1)

  (ii) Give the name of a possible composer.

  ....   (2)

(Total 16 marks)

Question 2: Comparisons 19

Test 4   **Tracks 31 & 32**

The following questions require you to compare and contrast TWO excerpts of music. The music for Excerpt A is on Track 31. The music for Excerpt B is on Track 32.

The excerpts are taken from different sections of the same sacred work with Latin text.

Translations: He has thrown down the powerful from their thrones and has lifted up the lowly. / He has come to the aid of his servant Israel, remembering his mercy [to Abraham and his descendants].

> **Note:** In answering (a) and (b), concentrate on the first part of Excerpt A (up to the beginning of a long rest for the tenor soloist at 1 minute 6 seconds) and the whole of Excerpt B.

(a) Underline the word TRUE or FALSE as appropriate below.

    (i) Only Excerpt A begins with wind instruments.   TRUE   FALSE   (1)

    (ii) Only Excerpt B has echo effects.   TRUE   FALSE   (1)

    (iii) Melisma is used more frequently in Excerpt B than in Excerpt A.   TRUE   FALSE   (1)

    (iv) Only Excerpt B uses imitation.   TRUE   FALSE   (1)

(b) Both excerpts include parts for solo tenor and for accompanying continuo instruments. Give **four** other similarities. You may identify specific continuo instruments that play in both excerpts.

    ....

    ....

    ....

    .... (4)

(c) Identify any significant **differences** between Excerpt A and Excerpt B not already mentioned. You may refer to instrumentation and types of voices used, melody, rhythm, and any other features you notice.

    ....

    ....

    ....

    ....

    ....

    .... (6)

(d) (i) In which of the following time spans were the excerpts composed?

             1550–80   1600–30   1650–80   1700–30   1750–80   (1)

    (ii) Which one of the following composers wrote both excerpts?

             Bach   Haydn   Monteverdi   Purcell   Taverner   (1)

(Total 16 marks)

20 Question 2: Comparisons

Test 5   **Tracks 33 & 34**

The following questions require you to compare and contrast TWO excerpts of music. The music for Excerpt A is on Track 33. The music for Excerpt B is on Track 34.

The excerpts are the openings of two orchestral works by the same composer.

(a) Underline the word TRUE or FALSE as appropriate below.

    (i)   Trills are heard only in Excerpt A.   TRUE   FALSE   **(1)**

    (ii) Pizzicato is used in Excerpt B only.   TRUE   FALSE   **(1)**

    (iii) Both excerpts use triplets in the accompaniment.   TRUE   FALSE   **(1)**

    (iv) A muted trumpet is heard only in Excerpt A.   TRUE   FALSE   **(1)**

(b) Give **four** similarities between the two excerpts. You may, for example, refer to rhythm, tonality and instrumentation.

....

....

....

.... **(4)**

(c) Identify any significant **differences** between the excerpts not already mentioned. Refer to melody, rhythm, instrumentation and tempo, but do not repeat information covered in question (a).

....

....

....

....

....

.... **(6)**

(d) (i) To which of the following time spans do both excerpts belong? Underline your answer.

       1800–40   1840–80   1880–1920   1920–60   **(1)**

   (ii) Which one of the following composers wrote both excerpts? Underline your answer.

       Beethoven   Brahms   Mahler   Tchaikovsky   Wagner   **(1)**

(Total 16 marks)

Test 6   **Tracks 35 & 36**

The following questions require you to compare and contrast TWO excerpts of music. The music for Excerpt A is on Track 35. The music for Excerpt B is on Track 36.

Both excerpts come from the same large-scale choral work with Latin text.

Translation of the main section of each excerpt: Which once you promised to Abraham and his descendants.

(a) Underline the word TRUE or FALSE as appropriate below.

    (i) An organ is used at the beginning of Excerpt B only.   TRUE   FALSE   **(1)**

    (ii) A tambourine is heard near the beginning of both excerpts.   TRUE   FALSE   **(1)**

    (iii) Both excerpts are in simple quadruple time.   TRUE   FALSE   **(1)**

    (iv) Vocal parts are conjunct in the opening bars of both excerpts.   TRUE   FALSE   **(1)**

(b) Each excerpt begins with an introductory section (about 30 seconds long in Excerpt A and about 10 seconds long in Excerpt B). Identify **two** differences in the vocal and instrumental forces. Avoid repeating any point covered in question (a).

    ....

    .... **(2)**

(c) What is the principal **similarity** between the two excerpts, apart from the use of vocal and orchestral forces and a Latin text? Listen to the passages which follow the introductory sections.

    .... **(1)**

(d) Compare and contrast the passages that follow the introductory sections, with reference to rhythm, melody, textures, and the tonality of the ending.

    ....

    ....

    ....

    ....

    ....

    .... **(6)**

(e) (i) Suggest a possible year of composition.

        .... **(1)**

    (ii) Suggest the name of **one** possible composer.

        .... **(2)**

                                                                                          (Total 16 marks)

Question 3: General Test of Aural Perception

Introduction

➤ First of all, make sure you know what the questions could involve. Besides the requirements for AS level, you may be asked to identify such chromatic chords as the augmented 6th and Neapolitan 6th, and modulations to any of the keys listed below, in the sixth paragraph.

➤ You will be working from a skeleton score. As with all the other questions on this paper, take care to manage the time at your disposal. To help you navigate your way around the question, the music on the CD will be divided into a number of tracks, indicated on the skeleton score, so that you can find your way quickly to the portion of the work upon which you wish to concentrate.

➤ Option (a) requires you to locate the whereabouts of three musical quotations. Don't forget to look at the clefs. Notice also if there are any internal clues regarding tonality, e.g. accidentals indicating a modulation to the dominant **may** mean that the extract will appear later rather than earlier.

➤ Option (b) requires you to notate a rhythm. No initial clue will be given concerning the number of notes, so it may help to place a dot on the skeleton score for each sound you hear before going on to establish the position of bar-lines and precise note-lengths.

➤ Option (c) requires you to add pitches to a given rhythm, which indicates the exact number of pitches to be notated. Take account of the context, i.e. at what pitch the preceding music stops and subsequently resumes. If you are not sure what is going on, try to decide whether the music moves by step, or whether it spells out harmonic or triadic patterns.

➤ Question (d) requires you to identify tonalities and chords. Identify the key of the opening and work out the related keys (dominant, subdominant, their relative majors/minors, the relative major/minor of the tonic, the tonic major/minor) before you begin your analysis. It may be that you are not certain of what you hear, but always remember you can predict or anticipate likely modulations and chord progressions on the basis of your theoretical knowledge.

When describing chords, it may sometimes help to feel the effects of cadence, i.e. incomplete imperfect, complete perfect, unexpected interrupted or church 'Amen' plagal. Use Test 1 as a means of developing a sense of whether a chord is a 7th or an augmented 6th. Notice how the augmented 6th will most frequently move to a dominant, often giving a half-close/imperfect feel, while the 7th will resolve, however fleetingly.

➤ Question (e) requires you to write a brief commentary on the music. If you are not sure about a particular fact, it is still worth stating it, providing of course you do not contradict yourself in the process. Here are some suggestions about the kind of information that examiners tend to look for:

Rhythm: Are the note-lengths even or are there dotted rhythms? Are there scotch snaps (Lombardic rhythms), hemiolas or syncopations?

Melody: Does it move by step or by leap? Is the range wide or narrow? Does the melody lie mainly in a high or low part of the range? Is it diatonic or chromatic? Is there any ornamentation? Does it involve sequence or repetition? How long are the phrases? Are they balanced?

Harmony: Is it consonant or are there dissonances, perhaps arising from the presence of suspensions and 7ths? Does it move by functional progressions? Are there cadences? Are there any pedal points? If so, are they in the bass or inverted (i.e. in an upper part)? Are they tonic or dominant? Are there any other features, such as tierce de Picardie, false relation or circle of 5ths?

Tonality: Is the extract in a major or minor key? Are there any modulations? Are there sudden shifts of key? Maybe there are modal inflections, e.g. flattened 7ths?

Texture: Are any parts of the music monophonic (single line) or in octaves (try to differentiate between the two)? Are there any contrapuntal passages? If so, is the counterpoint free or imitative (canonic, fugal)? Is the music chordal? Is there any melody-dominated homophony? Are there any examples of antiphony?

Instrumentation: This aspect should help you establish the historical period. For example, a harpsichord may well indicate baroque or early classical music. Harps, cor anglais and trombones should indicate music of a later date, although trombones with cornetti would indicate late renaissance or early baroque music.

Date: Be precise. An answer such as '1600s' or '18th century' is too wide to be helpful.

24 Question 3: General Test of Aural Perception

Test 1 Tracks 37–39

This test is based on a single, continuous piece of music.
Attempt ANY TWO from (a), (b) and (c). You must answer both (d) and (e).
The skeleton score is on pages 26–27.

(a) Where do you hear the following musical fragments? The fragments are not necessarily shown in the order in which they are heard.

(i)

The fragment begins in bar .... (2)

(ii)

The fragment begins in bar .... (2)

(iii)

The fragment begins in bar .... (2)

(b) Complete the **rhythm only** of the melody from bar 13, fifth quaver beat, to bar 15, first quaver beat. You may work in rough on the skeleton score, but must copy your answer onto the stave below.

(6)

(c) Add the **pitches** of the upper treble part from the last three semiquavers of bar 23 to the first quaver of bar 25. The rhythm is provided for you. You may work in rough on the skeleton score, but you must copy your answer onto the stave below.

(6)

(d) (i) Identify the chords indicated in bars 6, 8, 15 and 17.

bar 6 .... (1)

bar 8 .... (1)

bar 15 .... (1)

bar 17 .... (1)

(ii) Identify the key of bars 16–17. .... **(1)**

(iii) Identify the key of bars 26–27. .... **(1)**

(iv) Name the type of dissonance at bar 10, first quaver.

.... **(1)**

(v) What compositional device is used at bars 11–13?

.... **(1)**

(e) (i) Write a short commentary on this music. You may write in note form, bullet points or continuous prose. Mention any significant features of the music, for example, texture, form, harmony, rhythm and melodic style.

....

....

....

....

....

....

....

.... **(8)**

(ii) This is the second movement of a four-movement work. What type of work is this?

.... **(1)**

(iii) Place the music in its social and historical context by indicating a possible year of composition, who wrote the music, and for what performance circumstances.

....

....

.... **(3)**

(Total 32 marks)

Question 3: General Test of Aural Perception

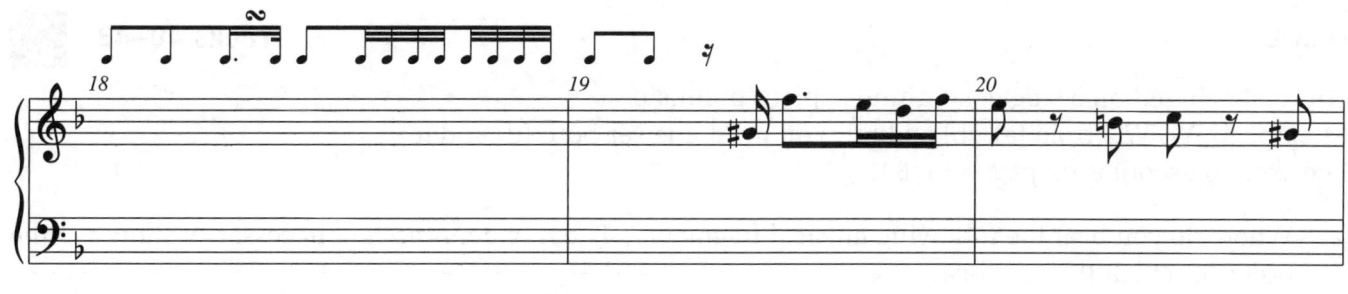

Question 3: General Test of Aural Perception

Test 2

Tracks 40–43

This test is based on a single, continuous piece of music.
Attempt ANY TWO from (a), (b) and (c). You must answer both (d) and (e).
The skeleton score is on pages 30–31.

(a) Where do you hear the following musical fragments? The fragments are not necessarily shown in the order in which they are heard.

> **Advice:** In this test, don't spend a long time searching for any of the musical fragments in the early part of the excerpt. Concentrate on Track 43!

(i)

The fragment begins in bar .... (2)

(ii)

The fragment begins in bar .... (2)

(iii)

The fragment begins in bar .... (2)

(b) Complete the **rhythm only** of the melody from bar 12, second quaver beat, to the end of bar 15. You may work in rough on the skeleton score, but you must copy your answer onto the stave below.

> **Advice:** There are ornaments in bar 13 (first quaver beat), bar 14 (second quaver beat) and bar 15 (first quaver beat). Do not notate these ornaments – simply write down the underlying note values. So, for example, if you hear a mordent on a quaver, just write down the quaver.

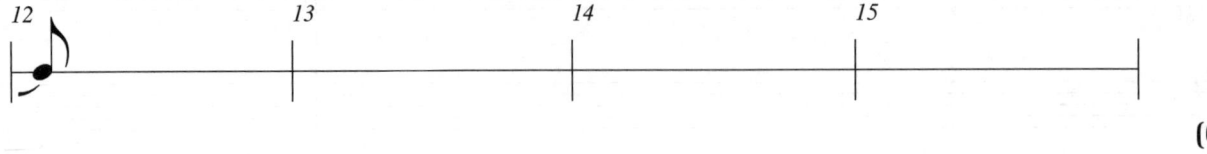

(6)

(c) Add the **pitches** of the melody from bar 23, last semiquaver beat, to the end of bar 26. The rhythm is provided for you. You may work in rough on the skeleton score, but you must copy your answer onto the stave below.

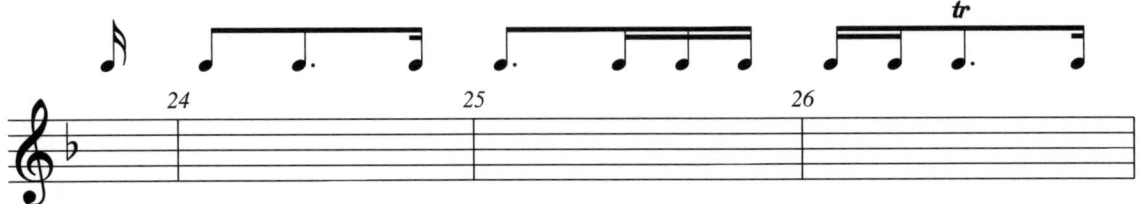

(6)

(d) (i) Identify the chords marked in bars 4, 34 and 35. All are in F major.

bar 4 .... (1)

bar 34 .... (1)

bar 35 .... (1)

(ii) Identify the cadence in bar 59. .... (1)

(iii) Identify the dissonance at the beginning of bar 59.

.... (1)

(iv) Identify the key at bars 24–27. .... (1)

(v) Complete the following with the names of two different keys.

In bars 50–52 the music passes through .... From the second half of bar 57 to the end, the music is in .... (2)

(e) (i) Write a short commentary on this music. You may write in note form, bullet points or continuous prose. Mention any significant features of the music, for example, instrumentation, texture, harmony, rhythm, melodic style, and structure.

....
....
....
....
....
....
....
.... (8)

(ii) The excerpt you have heard is a complete movement. From what kind of work do you think it has been taken? What evidence points to its being the second movement rather than the first or the last?

....
.... (2)

(iii) Place the music in its historical context by indicating a possible year of composition and who wrote the music.

....
.... (2)

(Total 32 marks)

Question 3: General Test of Aural Perception

32 Question 3: General Test of Aural Perception

Test 3 Track 44–47

This test is based on a single, continuous piece of music.
Attempt ANY TWO from (a), (b) and (c). You must answer both (d) and (e).
The skeleton score is on pages 34–35.

(a) Where do you hear the following musical fragments? The fragments are not necessarily shown in the order in which they are heard.

(i)

   The fragment begins in bar .... (2)

(ii)

   The fragment begins in bar .... (2)

(iii)

   The fragment begins in bar .... (2)

(b) Complete the rhythm only of the melody from bar 15, fourth note to the end of bar 16. You may work in rough on the skeleton score, but must copy your answer onto the stave below.

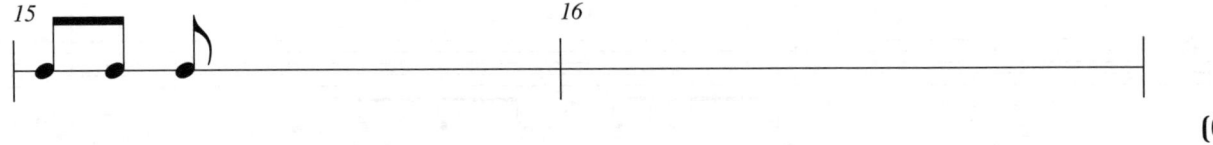

(6)

(c) Add the pitches of the violin part from bar 7, fourth note, to bar 8, sixth note. The rhythm is provided for you. You may work in rough on the skeleton score, but must copy your answer onto the stave below.

(6)

(d) (i) Identify the two chords at bar 2, beats 3 and 4 respectively.

   bar 2, beat 3   .... (1)

   bar 2, beat 4   .... (1)

   (ii) Identify the key from bar 4 to bar 5 (first beat).

   ....

   (1)

(iii) Identify the key touched on between bar 5, fourth quaver and bar 6, first quaver.

.... (1)

(iv) Identify precisely the type of dissonance used at bar 10, beat 1.

.... (1)

(v) Identify the three chords marked in bar 25. The key is D minor.

    1 .... (1)

    2 .... (1)

    3 .... (1)

(e) (i) Write a short commentary on this music. You may write in note form, bullet points or continuous prose. Mention any significant features of the music, for example, forces, rhythm, melody, harmony, tonality, texture and structure.

....

....

....

....

....

....

....

.... (8)

(ii) This is a fragment from a larger work. What sort of work is this?

.... (1)

(iii) Place the music in its social and historical context by indicating a possible year of composition, who wrote the music, and for what performance circumstances.

....

....

.... (3)

(Total 32 marks)

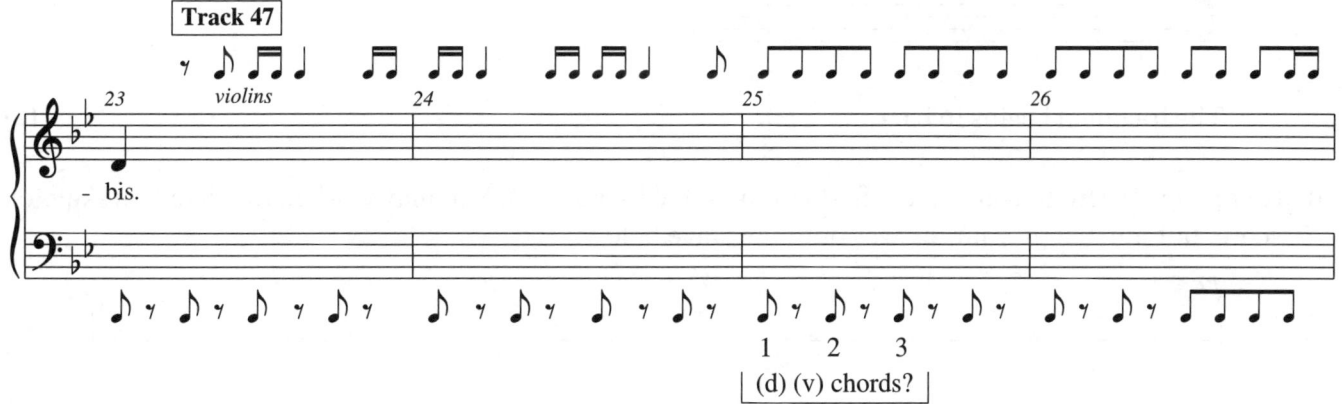
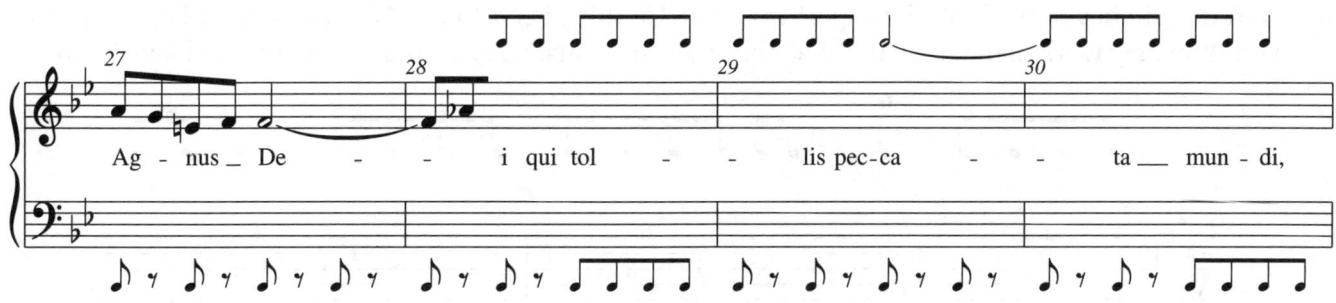
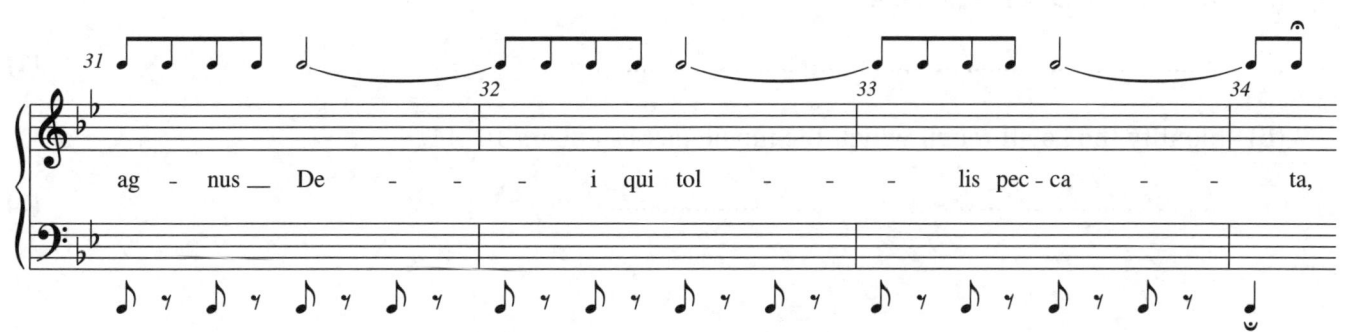

36 Question 3: General Test of Aural Perception

Test 4 Tracks 48–51

This test is based on a single, continuous piece of music.
Attempt ANY TWO from (a), (b) and (c). You must answer both (d) and (e).
The skeleton score in on pages 38–40.

(a) Where do you hear the following musical fragments? The fragments are not necessarily shown in the order in which they are heard.

(i)

  The fragment begins in bar .... (2)

(ii)

  The fragment begins in bar .... (2)

(iii)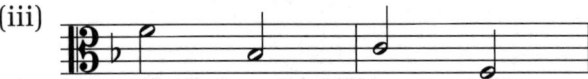

  The fragment begins in bar .... (2)

(b) Complete the **rhythm** only of the first violin part of bars 19–20. You may work in rough on the skeleton score, but must copy your answer onto the stave below.

(6)

(c) Add the **pitches** of the first violin part from bar 15, third beat, to bar 17. The rhythm is provided for you. You may work in rough on the skeleton score, but must copy your answer onto the stave below.

(6)

(d) (i) Identify the cadence at bar 4.

  .... (1)

  (ii) Identify the key through which the music passes at bars 10–11.

  .... (1)

(iii) Identify the cadence at bar 12.

.... **(1)**

(iv) Identify the **four** chords marked with arrows in bars 26–27.

1. .... 2. .... 3. .... 4. .... **(4)**

(v) Identify the key of bars 50–52.

.... **(1)**

(e) (i) Write a short commentary on this music. You may write in note form, bullet points or continuous prose. Mention any significant features of the music, for example, texture, form, harmony, rhythm and melodic style.

....

....

....

....

....

....

....

.... **(8)**

(ii) This is the first movement of a four-movement work. What type of work is this?

.... **(1)**

(iii) Place the music in its social and historical context by indicating a possible year of composition, who wrote the music, and for what performance circumstances.

....

....

.... **(3)**

(Total 32 marks)

Question 3: General Test of Aural Perception

Track 48

Allegro

(d) (i) cadence

(d) (ii) key

Track 49

(d) (iii) cadence

(c) pitches

Question 3: General Test of Aural Perception 39

(b) rhythm

Track 50

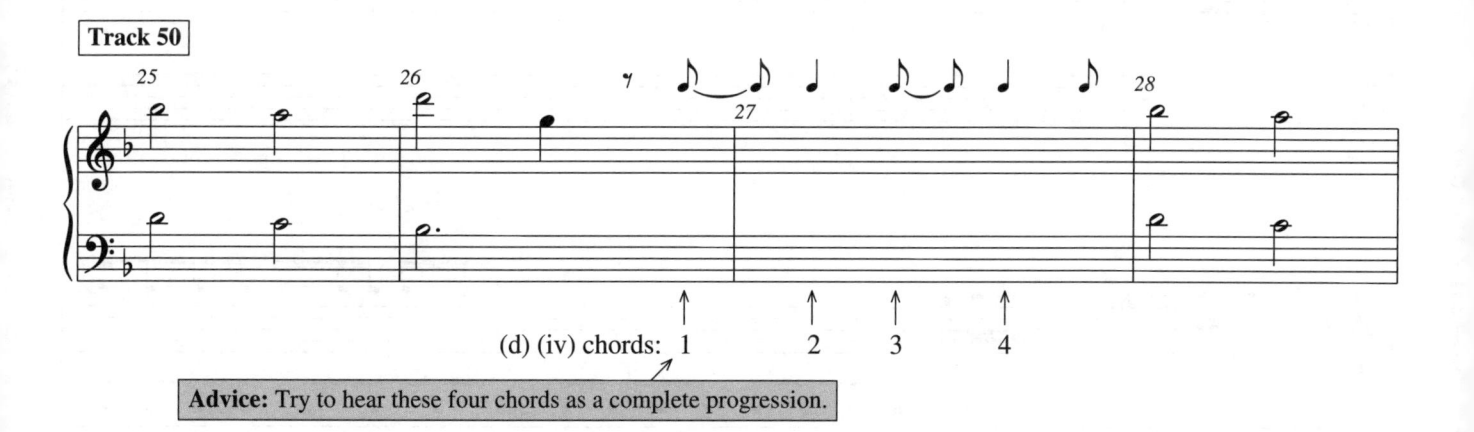

(d) (iv) chords: 1 2 3 4

Advice: Try to hear these four chords as a complete progression.

Question 3: General Test of Aural Perception

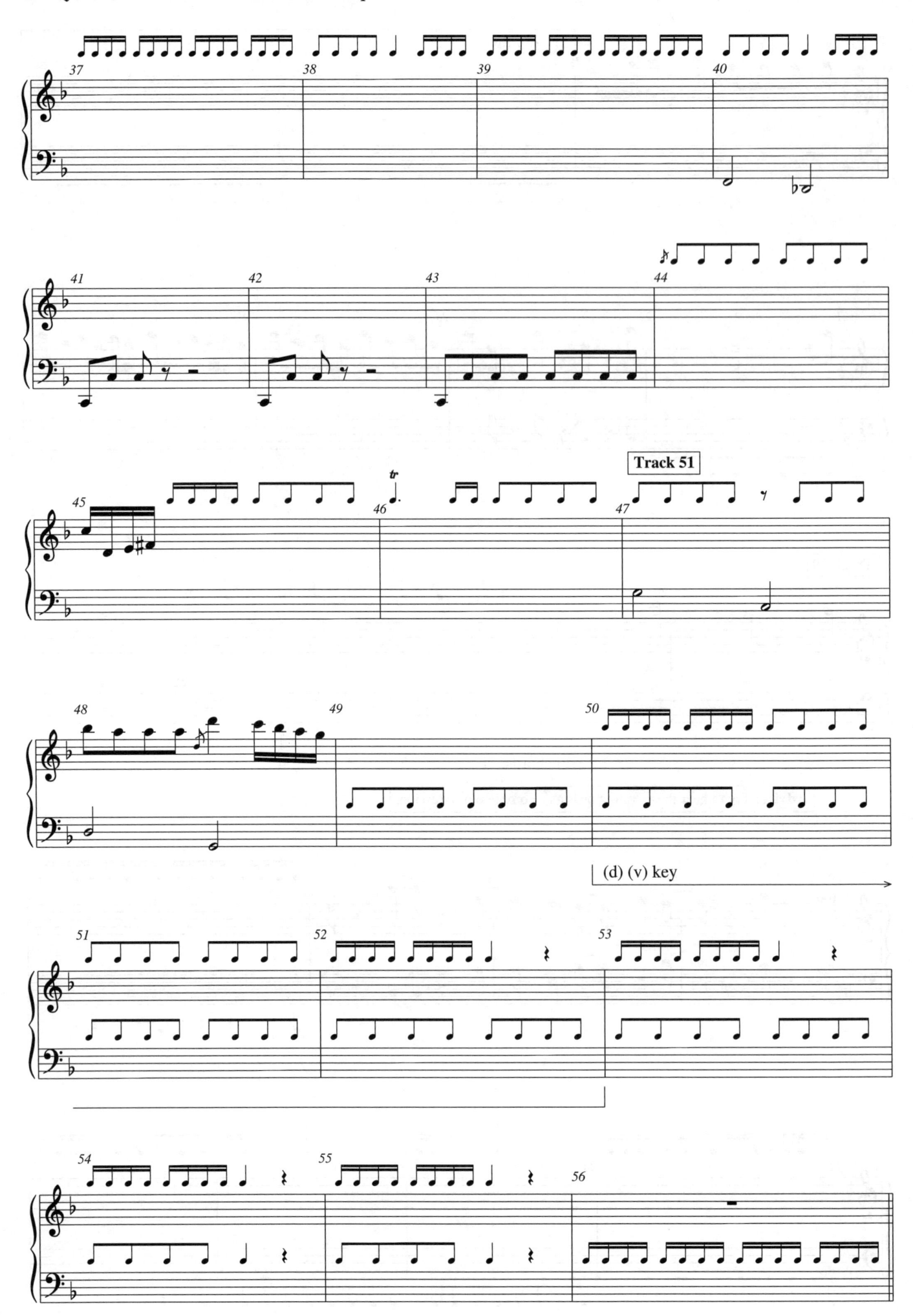

Track 51

(d) (v) key

Question 3: General Test of Aural Perception

Test 5 **Tracks 52–55**

This test is based on a single, continuous piece of music.
Attempt ANY TWO from sections (a), (b) and (c). You must answer both (d) and (e).
The skeleton score is on pages 43–45.

(a) Where do you hear the following musical fragments? The fragments are not necessarily shown in the order in which they are heard.

(i)

The fragment is heard in bar .... (2)

(ii)

The fragment is heard in bar .... (2)

(iii)

The fragment is heard in bar .... (2)

(b) Complete the **rhythm only** of the violin part in bars 6–7. You may work in rough on the skeleton score, but must copy your answer onto the stave below.

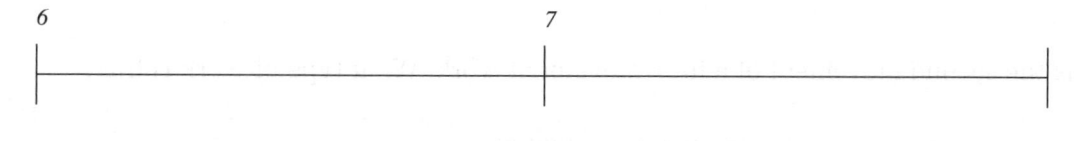

(6)

(c) Add the **pitches** of the violin part from the first note of bar 18 to the first note of bar 19. The rhythm is provided for you. You may work in rough on the skeleton score but you must copy your answer onto the stave below.

(6)

(d) (i) Complete the sentence below:

A tonic pedal begins in bar 17 and ends at bar .... , beat .... (1)

(ii) Identify the key at bars 20–21.

.... (1)

Question 3: General Test of Aural Perception

   (iii) Identify the key at bars 24–26.

   .... (1)

   (iv) Describe precisely the dissonance on the first beat of bar 31.

   .... (1)

   (v) Identify the **four** chords marked with arrows in bar 33.

   1. ....   2. ....   3. ....   4. .... (4)

(e) (i) Write a short commentary on this music. You may write in note form, bullet points or continuous prose. Mention any significant features of the music, for example, instrumentation, texture, form, harmony, rhythm and melodic style.

   ....

   ....

   ....

   ....

   ....

   ....

   ....

   .... (8)

   (ii) This is the second movement of a four-movement work. What type of work is this?

   .... (1)

   (iii) Place the music in its social and historical context by indicating a possible year of composition, who wrote the music, and for what performance circumstances.

   ....

   ....

   .... (3)

(Total 32 marks)

Question 3: General Test of Aural Perception

(c) pitches
18
19
20
(d) (ii) key
21
22
23

Track 54

24
25
(d) (iii) key
26
27
28
29
30
31
(d) (iv) dissonance

Question 3: General Test of Aural Perception

Track 55

(d) (v) chords: 1   2   3   4

Question 3: General Test of Aural Perception

Test 6 Tracks 56–59

This test is based on a single, continuous piece of music.
Attempt ANY TWO from sections (a), (b) and (c). You must answer both (d) and (e).
The skeleton score is on pages 48–49.

(a) Where do you hear the following musical fragments? The fragments are not necessarily shown in the order in which they are heard.

(i) [musical notation in bass clef]

The fragment begins in bar .... (2)

(ii) [musical notation in treble clef]

The fragment begins in bar .... (2)

(iii) [musical notation in treble clef]

The fragment is heard in bar .... (2)

(b) Complete the **rhythm only** of the violin from bar 5, beat 1, to bar 7, beat 1. You may work in rough on the skeleton score, but must copy your answer onto the stave below.

[empty staff with bar numbers 5, 6, 7]

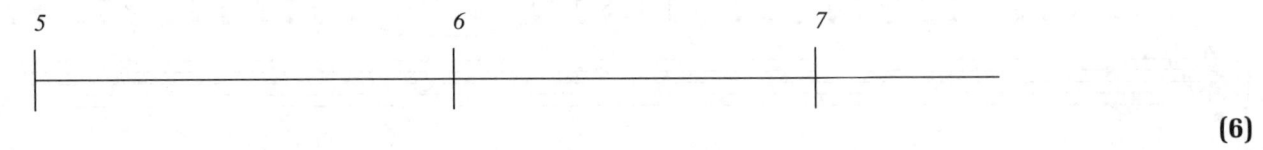

(6)

(c) Add the **pitches** of the top part in the piano from bar 23, third beat, to bar 25, first six notes. The rhythm is provided for you. You may work in rough on the skeleton score, but you must copy your answer onto the stave below.

[musical notation with bars 23, 24, 25]

(6)

(d) (i) Describe the chord in the piano part at bar 12, beat 3, and the device used simultaneously in the violin part to intensify the dissonance.

chord .... device .... (2)

(ii) Identify the key through which the music briefly passes at bars 14 and 15.

   .... (1)

(iii) Identify the chord at bars 25–26.

   .... (1)

(iv) Identify the key at the close of the extract.

   .... (1)

(v) Identify the **three** chords marked with arrows in bars 46–47.

   1. .... 2. .... 3. .... (3)

(e) (i) Write a short commentary on this music. You may write in note form, bullet points or continuous prose. Mention any significant features of the music, for example, instrumentation, texture, form, harmony, rhythm and melodic style.

   ....

   ....

   ....

   ....

   ....

   ....

   ....

   .... (8)

(ii) This is taken from the first movement of a three-movement work. What type of work is this?

   .... (1)

(iii) Place the music in its social and historical context by indicating a possible year of composition, who wrote the music, and for what performance circumstances.

   ....

   ....

   .... (3)

(Total 32 marks)

48 Question 3: General Test of Aural Perception

Question 3: General Test of Aural Perception

Answers and How to Mark Them

Note that in this mark scheme words or phrases in parentheses are not essential. Words that are underlined <u>are</u> essential. An oblique stroke (/) separates alternative correct solutions. No mark scheme is completely comprehensive so if you provide correct and relevant information that is not listed below, remember that it could still receive credit. Ask your teacher if in doubt.

Question 1: Context

Test 1

Excerpt A
Purcell's *The Indian Queen* was unfinished at the composer's death in 1695. It was a semi-opera, a type of play with musical episodes cultivated in England from about 1675 to 1710. Did you identify Purcell as the composer of this excerpt? If not, listen to some more of Purcell's music.

(i) air (1)
(ii) any year 1660–1700 (2) / 1700–50 (1)
(iii) Purcell / Blow / other composer active in late 17th- or early 18th-century England, including Handel (1)

Excerpt B
Beethoven's String Quartet in F minor, Op. 95, a serious and concentrated work, dates from 1810. The opening diminished 7th chords of the excerpt effect a link back to F minor from the second movement, which is in the distant key of D major. In his later music Beethoven often, as here, worked a short rhythmic pattern very hard: can you notate the recurring rhythm used here? The music is very characteristic of Beethoven: it is too violent for any earlier composer; on the other hand the harmonic style in particular marks it out as early 19th century rather than late 19th or 20th century.

(i) string quartet (1)
(ii) any year 1805–27 (2) / 1795–1804, 1828–40 (1)
(iii) Beethoven (1)

Excerpt C
John Tavener composed 'The Tiger' in 1987, two years after 'The Lamb', an item perhaps familiar to you from the Sacred Vocal Music area of study in *The New Anthology of Music*. The words of 'The Lamb' were taken from William Blake's *Songs of Innocence* (1789), whereas Blake's poem 'The Tyger' is from *Songs of Experience* (1794). You may find it interesting and useful to compare the two poems and their musical treatments.

(i) postmodern (2) / minimalist (1)
(ii) 1980–90 (1)
(iii) Tavener / Pärt (despite the English words) / other postmodern composer working in a similar style (1)

Test 2

Excerpt A
A Passion is a musical setting of the story of the sufferings and death of Jesus Christ as told in the Bible by one of the gospel writers, but usually it also includes settings of items by later writers which reflect on that story. Bach preferred recitative for the biblical narrative, and set many of the poetic texts as arias. His Passions include chorales, some of which you may have encountered when working on compositional techniques. Bach's *St John Passion* was first performed in Leipzig in 1724.

(i) recitative (1); aria (1). Note: because of the headings 'first piece' and 'second piece' in the question paper, your responses must be in the order shown (not 'aria', 'recitative').
(ii) any year 1710–50 (1)
(iii) J S Bach (1)

Excerpt B
The opera *The Rake's Progress* dates from 1947–51, and was Stravinsky's last great neo-classical work before his move towards serialism. Its neo-classicism includes the use of recitatives and arias in the manner of 18th-century opera (there is even a harpsichord), and some echoes of Mozart, but Stravinsky was not reorchestrating or building on specific 18th-century originals as he was in *Pulcinella*.

(i) neo-classicism (1)
(ii) any year 1930–60 (2) / 1920–29, 1961–71 (1)
(iii) Stravinsky / Britten / Tippett / other leading English opera composer of the mid 20th century (1)

Excerpt C
The recording you have heard was made in 1947 at a live performance in Carnegie Hall, New York. The American saxophone player Charlie Parker (1920–55) was a key figure in developing bop (or bebop as it can also be termed), along with Dizzy Gillespie (1917–93), the American jazz trumpeter, composer and bandleader. Both men, but especially Parker, were brilliant and much imitated improvisers.

(i) bop / bebop (2) / jazz (1)
(ii) 1940s (1). Accept instead 1930s *or* 1950s
(iii) Dizzy Gillespie / Charlie Parker (1). Note: you are asked simply for the name of either musician, and do not need to state the instrument played.

Test 3

Excerpt A
An oratorio by Handel entitled *Alexander's Feast*, which was based on John Dryden's *Ode for St Cecilia's Day*, was first performed in 1736. The concerto from which Excerpt A comes acquired its name because it was played between acts I and II of the oratorio: such use of instrumental music between the acts of oratorios was common in Handel's day.

(i) concerto grosso (1) Note: at A2, it is very unlikely that 'concerto' alone would receive any credit.
(ii) any year 1720–50 (2) / 1680–1719 (1)
(iii) Handel / any early 18th-century Italian or Italianate composer of concerti grossi for strings (such as Albinoni) (1). Do not accept J S Bach, whose style is more 'intense'.

Excerpt B
Tosca was first staged in Rome in 1900, and its music has been popular with great singers and with opera audiences ever since. Tosca herself is a famous singer, and in 'Vissi d'arte' tells of her devotion to art and love. In the 1990s Puccini's music reached new audiences when the Italian tenor Pavarotti popularised 'Nessun dorma' from Puccini's *Turandot*. If you thought our excerpt was by Verdi, listen to more by him and by Puccini, and note Puccini's often more striking use of the orchestra, and a style that frequently points ahead to the 20th century.

(i) opera (1)
(ii) 1890–1910 (1)
(iii) Puccini (2) / Verdi / other Italian operatic composer from the late 19th or early 20th century (1)

Excerpt C
Our recording of Bessie Smith singing 'Jail House Blues' was among the first she made, in 1923, with Irving Johns (piano). Bessie Smith (1894–1937), often known as queen or even empress of the blues on account of the wonderful expressiveness and intensity of her singing, made over 200 recordings, mostly in the 1920s. Her best-known recording in her own day was 'Back Water Blues' (1927) with James P Johnson on piano.

(i) blues (1)
(ii) 1920s (2) / 1910s *or* 1930s (1)
(iii) Bessie Smith (1)

Test 4

Excerpt A
This excerpt is the ending of the Magnificat, the closing item from Monteverdi's Vespers (published 1610). Featuring Monteverdi's full vocal and instrumental forces, it has some imposing homophonic writing before the more complex contrapuntal and melismatic Amen. This is an example of the early baroque concertato style, cultivated most especially in Venice. Imagine the impact that this would have made on early 17th-century listeners previously accustomed to unaccompanied renaissance polyphony!

(i) church service / Vespers (of the BVM) / sacred / religious (1)
(ii) any year 1600–20 (2) / 1590–99, 1621–50 (1)
(iii) Monteverdi / Gabrieli / Schütz (who composed some music with Latin text) / other early 17th-century composer who wrote in the early baroque concertato style (1)

Excerpt B
Liszt was the one of the most exciting and original composers of the 19th century, and an outstanding piano virtuoso (he set out to do for the piano what Paganini had done for the violin). Even today few pianists want to play works such as this 'transcendental' study in public. The pianist who made it sound so manageable on the recording was Jenö Jandó.

(i) piano recital (1) concert hall / public performance (both too vague) (0)
(ii) 1851 (1)
(iii) Liszt (2) / Chopin (1)

Excerpt C
The album *Stage Struck* by Rory Gallagher (1949–95), which includes 'Shin Kicker' (1978), was compiled from a number of live recordings made during concerts on a world tour in 1979 and 1980.

(i) live (1) at a rock concert (1)
(ii) hard rock (1)
(iii) any year 1970–90 (1)

Test 5

Excerpt A
William Byrd was the outstanding English composer at the end of the 16th and beginning of the 17th century. He excelled in sacred music, but made a major contribution to keyboard music and music for viols. A pavan or pavane was a renaissance court dance of Italian origin in duple metre with two, three or four sections, each repeated. Locate the pavanes from *The New Anthology of Music* and compare them with Byrd's piece.

(i) any year 1560–1630 (1)
(ii) (consort of) viols (1); use of pavan (1); modal / pre-tonal harmonic style (1). Max. 2
(iii) Byrd (1)

Excerpt B
Country music has its principal roots in the southern states of the USA, and incorporates elements from 19th-century popular music, blues and gospel songs,

although it is indebted also to earlier folk songs and dances from the British Isles. Dolly Parton (born 1946), who recorded her song 'Coat of Many Colors' in the early 1970s, is one of a number of American singers whose work has brought what was originally a localised style of music to massive audiences worldwide.

(i) country (and western) (1)
(ii) any year 1970–79 (2) / 1960–69, 1980–89 (1)
(iii) (Dolly) Parton (1)

Excerpt C
'La Vallée des cloches' ('The Valley of Bells') is the last of five pieces named *Miroirs* which Ravel composed in 1904–05, and is a reminder that impressionist pieces were not the sole preserve of Debussy. Indeed, Debussy may even have been influenced by 'La Vallée des cloches' when he composed 'Et la Lune descend sur le temple qui fut' from *Images* (1907).

(i) impressionist (1)
(ii) any year 1900–15 (2) / 1890–99, 1916–37 (1)
(iii) Ravel / Debussy (1)

Test 6
Excerpt A
'Lauda mater ecclesia', a motet by Orlande de Lassus (c. 1530–94) in which plainsong and unaccompanied vocal polyphonic writing alternate, was published in 1597: its precise date is unknown. Lassus, who was widely known and admired in late 16th-century Europe, wrote an enormous number of works both for the church (mostly with Latin, but occasionally with German texts) and for secular use (with Italian, French and German texts).

(i) plainsong / plainchant (1)
(ii) sacred polyphony (1)
(iii) any year 1550–1600 (2) / 1530–49, 1601–20 (1)

Excerpt B
Schoenberg composed the three piano pieces of *Drei Klavierstücke*, Op. 11 in 1909. These pieces precede *Pierrot Lunaire* (from which you may know 'Der kranke Mond') by three years, and were among the first that completely rejected traditional functional harmony and tonality. They are among Schoenberg's expressionist works, with a new emotional intensity that sometimes resulted in extreme and abrupt contrasts. They are not serial: serialism did not develop until the early 1920s.

(i) expressionism (1). Note: you can hear more 'colourful' examples of expressionism in other works by Schoenberg composed around 1910, including *Pierrot Lunaire* and *Erwärtung*.
(ii) any year 1900–19 (2) / 1920–51 (1)
(iii) Schoenberg / Berg (1)

Excerpt C
'Stardust' was recorded in 1943. The track begins with the following spoken announcement, which we did not include for obvious reasons: 'This is Captain Glenn Miller speaking for the [US] Army Air Forces Training Command Orchestra, and we hope you soldiers of the Allied Forces enjoy these V-discs that we're making just for you.' The orchestra was much larger than the bands with which Miller had recorded in the 1930s and early 1940s, with 20 string players in addition to the more 'conventional' trumpets, trombones, saxes, etc.

(i) swing / big band (jazz) (2) / jazz (1)
(ii) 1940s (1)
(iii) Glenn Miller / Jimmy Dorsey / Artie Shaw / other contemporary bandleader (1)

Test 7
Excerpt A
Elgar composed his *Imperial March* for the Diamond Jubilee of Queen Victoria in 1897. Like the *Pomp and Circumstance* March No. 1 (with its 'Land of Hope and Glory' Trio) this is a concert march for symphony orchestra rather than a piece to accompany the marching of troops. Elgar flourished when the British Empire was at its height, and much of his music has a grandeur that seems to mirror Britain's international status.

(i) concert march (1)
(ii) any year 1890–1910 (2) / 1880–89, 1911–34 (1)
(iii) Elgar (1)

Excerpt B
Schoenberg's *Suite*, Op. 25 dates mainly from 1923, and employs the 12-note serial method throughout. Most of its movements are in dance forms – the excerpt you have just heard is the Trio of a Menuett – but the language of the music is not neoclassical in the manner of Stravinsky's *Pulcinella* (1919–20). Can you hear the canonic writing in Schoenberg's Trio?

(i) serialism (1)
(ii) any year 1920–51 (2) / 1905–19 (1)
(iii) Schoenberg / Webern / Berg (1)

Excerpt C
Neil Sedaka (born 1939) came to prominence in the late 1950s with his song 'Stupid Cupid', and he became a 'teen idol' in the early 1960s with songs such as 'Happy Birthday, Sweet Sixteen', 'Calendar Girl' and 'Breaking Up is Hard to Do'. After the 'British invasion' of the USA by the Beatles and the Rolling Stones, Sedaka's music was less popular, but he continued songwriting, and later gained considerable success in Britain, other European countries, and Japan.

(i) pop (1). Note: 'popular music' is too wide-ranging a term.

(ii) any year 1955–65 (2) / 1966–80 (1)
(iii) Neil Sedaka (1)

Test 8

Excerpt A

'Wir Christenleut', one of the chorale preludes (or organ chorales) from the so-called Kirnberger collection, is commonly ascribed to J S Bach. The 'Wir Christenleut' melody appears in the bass (played on the pedals by the organist's feet), under two-part imitative writing performed on the manuals (keyboards). The opening motif, derived from the melody itself, is widely used, sometimes in inversion. For four-part harmonisations of the melody, see *Bach: 371 Harmonized Chorales*, edited by A Riemenschneider (New York, 1941), items 55, 321 and 360.

(i) chorale prelude / organ chorale (2) / chorale / (organ) voluntary (1)
(ii) 1710–50 (1)
(iii) (J S) Bach (1) / other 17th- or 18th-century German composer of chorale preludes / Buxtehude (1)

Excerpt B

Haydn's symphonies Nos. 6, 7 and 8 – 'Le Matin' ('Morning'), 'Le Midi' ('Noon') and 'Le Soir' ('Evening') – were composed in 1761 for Prince Paul Anton Esterházy, a member of a rich and powerful family for whom Haydn worked for many years. The works demonstrated brilliantly the talents of the prince's band of about 15, many of them expert players. Compare this cheerful example of the early classical style with the more serious Symphony No. 26 in D minor from *The New Anthology*.

(i) symphony (1)
(ii) any year 1750–75 (2) / 1776–1800 (1)
(iii) Haydn / Mozart / J C Bach / other late 18th-century composer of symphonies (1)

Excerpt C

Thelonious Monk (1917–82) was one of the great jazz innovators and his music has often been misunderstood. People sometimes criticised his piano playing as lacking in technique, but it is clear from this recording that it was perfectly adequate to express his musical thoughts. The recording was made by the Thelonious Monk Quartet in 1948. The title 'Epistrophy' may or may not be connected with the word 'epistrophe', a rhetorical term that refers to ending a succession of phrases or sentences with the same word(s).

(i) modern (1) jazz (1)
(ii) any year 1940–59 (1)
(iii) Thelonious Monk (1)

Question 2: Comparisons

Test 1

These extracts are taken from Elgar's Symphony No. 1 in A♭, Op. 55 (1908). The first is the introduction to the first movement, and the second the coda of the finale. The work was dedicated to Hans Richter, then conductor of the Hallé orchestra in Manchester, who gave the first performance on 3 December 1908. One of Elgar's most successful works, it was performed more than a hundred times in its first year alone.

(a) (i) TRUE; (ii) TRUE; (iii) FALSE; (iv) TRUE; (4)
(b) A has a shorter intro (1) (NB no further marks for saying B has a longer intro!), with a single note (½) tonic (1) on string basses (½) and timpani roll (½). In contrast B has a wide-ranging harmonic progression (1) for full orchestra (1). Max. 3
(c) same melody (1); same key (1); allow very similar tempo (1). A has two-part melody and bass (1) with occasional additional voice in middle of texture (1), while B is for full orchestra (1) with elaborate flourishes (1). Max. 4
(d) A remains at same tempo (½); B has faster section (½). Melodic differences (½), e.g. the original high A♭ omitted in B (½). A has a brief link based on broken chords (½), while B has a link built on a dominant pedal (½). A has irregular phrase lengths (½); B uses regular two-bar phrases in the faster section (½). A fades at end (½); B finishes loudly (½). Max. 3
(e) (i) 1890–1910 (1); (ii) Elgar (1)

Test 2

These extracts, from the finale of Sibelius's Fifth Symphony, Op. 82 (1919), are the exposition and recapitulation of (mainly) the second subject. This distinctive theme was linked by the composer to the sight of 16 swans in flight ('One of my greatest experiences! Lord God, that beauty!'). Notice particularly the thrilling tertiary shift from E♭ to C major in the exposition, and the masterly control of tempo, especially the way in which the music moves to a slower speed in the recapitulation.

(a) (i) TRUE; (ii) FALSE; (iii) TRUE; (iv) FALSE; (4)
(b) tremolandi in both (1); both anticipate next theme in bass/have longer notes in bass (1). They are in different keys (1), B uses muted strings (1)/is softer (½). Max. 3
(c) YES (1)
(d) tempo is maintained in A (1), whereas B progressively slows down (1). Different key relationships are used, A moving from E♭ to C, i.e. tertiary modulation (1), whereas B moves from G♭ to E♭ minor (1), before a final turn to the major.

Main theme appears on horns in A (1), strings in B (1). Augmented bass melody arco in A (1), pizz in B (1). A finishes in major (1), B in the minor (1). Max. 6

(e) (i) 1919 (1); (ii) Sibelius (1)

Test 3

These extracts come from the first movement of Beethoven's Concerto for Piano, Violin and Cello in C, Op. 56 (c. 1804). The first excerpt is the opening statement of the first subject, and the second the soloists' exposition (and expansion) of the same material.

(a) (i) TRUE; (ii) TRUE; (iii) TRUE; (iv) TRUE; (4)

(b) similarities: same tempo (1), same key (1); differences: cello and basses (1), playing monophonically (1) in first excerpt; in second excerpt, the theme is played by a solo cello (1), an octave higher (1), supported throughout by orchestra (1), the melody line now modified to become more sustained (1). Max. 3

(c) Excerpt A: prolonged passage built on tonic triad (1); leading to orchestral tutti (1), and a modulation to dominant at close (1).
Excerpt B: after cello entry, the theme is played in dominant (1) by solo violin (1) and then again in tonic (1) by the piano (1). Before the piano entry, the solo strings play unaccompanied (1) in parallel 10ths (1) and 6ths (1). Max. 5

(d) concerto (1)

(e) (i) any year 1790–1820 (1); (ii) Beethoven (2); Haydn / Mozart (1)

Test 4

These two extracts are taken from the Magnificat in Monteverdi's Vespers, (published in Venice in 1610). Although Monteverdi was appointed to the post of maestro di cappella at St. Mark's only in 1613, the Vespers provide some of the finest examples of the early baroque concertato style associated with Venetian composers. These examples also demonstrate the way in which Monteverdi combined sacred cantus firmus technique (the plainsong melody in long notes sung by tenor) and more complex vocal and instrumental elaborations typical of his operatic style.

(a) (i) TRUE; (ii) FALSE; (iii) TRUE; (iv) TRUE (antiphony is used in Excerpt A); (4)

(b) both tenor parts have essentially the same melody/cantus firmus (1) in long notes (1), with syllabic word-setting (1), except in the final phrase (1). In both extracts the continuo instruments are cello, organ and chitarrone/theorbo/large or bass lute (1). Max. 4

(c) Excerpt A: cornetts (1) play in 3rds, as do violins (1). Dotted rhythms are employed (1). Melodic lines frequently move in step/avoid large leaps (1), there are even complete scales (1), and measured 'trills' (1).
Excerpt B: two soprano voices (1), in imitation at first (no credit because of section (a)) then in free counterpoint (1). A slightly larger range of intervals is used here (1). Max. 6

(d) (i) 1600–30 (1); (ii) Monteverdi (1)

Test 5

These excerpts are taken from the first movements of Mahler's Third Symphony (completed 1896) and Seventh Symphony (1904–05). The first excerpt contains one of the most famous solo passages in the trombone repertory. The second excerpt reflects the expansion of Mahler's harmonic language in his later works. This passage is noticeably more chromatic and tonally wayward (the opening chord is an added 6th, and later parts of the symphony employ quartal harmony. i.e. chords of superimposed 4ths).

(a) (i) FALSE; (ii) TRUE; (iii) FALSE; (iv) TRUE; (4)

(b) minor (1), with some references to tonic major (1); dotted rhythms (1) and triplets (1); variations in tempo (1), tremolando (1), prominent solo for brass instruments (1). Max. 4

(c) Excerpt A is in triple metre (1) as opposed to the (mainly) quadruple metre in Excerpt B (1); it is mainly melody-dominated homophony (1), whereas there is a mixture of textures, e.g. melody-dominated homophony at start (1) moving into contrapuntal writing in Excerpt B (1); melody line in Excerpt A is retained in trombone throughout (1), whereas it moves from tenor horn to woodwinds (sometimes doubling strings) in Excerpt B (1). In Excerpt A, the melody revolves around the dominant (at first) (1), whereas that of Excerpt B ranges more freely (1), and is more chromatic in general (1). Max. 6

(d) (i) 1880–1920 (1); (ii) Mahler (1)

Test 6

These extracts come from the Offertorium of Britten's War Requiem (1962), on either side of a setting of one of Wilfred Owen's war poems. The change of mode, inversions and generally muted atmosphere of the second extract reflect Britten's ironic response to the grim message of the war poem.

(a) (i) TRUE; (ii) FALSE; (iii) FALSE; (iv) FALSE; (4)

(b) Excerpt A: full orchestra (1) alternates with homophonic (½) chorus (½)
Excerpt B: monophonic (1) low strings (1). Max. 2

(c) same melody / conjunct movement / same metre and rhythmic patterns (1)

(d) rhythm: compound time in both (1) with hemiola (1); melody: conjunct in both (1), but in Excerpt B the initial rising subject is heard inverted (1); the subject is fragmented (1); textures: fugal (1), with stretto (1), chords built up (1); textures inverted, so that low voices in Excerpt A are replaced with high voices in Excerpt B (1). Fewer instruments in B (1).

A finishes in a major key (1) and B on a minor chord (1). Max. 6

(e) (i) any year 1950–76 (1)

(ii) Britten (2), Walton / Tippett / Vaughan Williams (1)

Question 3: General Test of Aural Perception

Test 1

This extract is the opening of the slow movement from Beethoven's Piano Sonata No. 7, Op. 10, No. 3. It was composed in 1797, not long before the Septet, Op. 20 (*The New Anthology of Music*, No. 17). It forms a fascinating contrast with the later work, indicating that some of Beethoven's most intense earlier works were reserved for the piano. Notice how the melody line is intensified by appoggiaturas, and how the harmonic tension is kept high by the plentiful use of diminished 7th and augmented 6th chords. Keep listening to this excerpt, even after you have worked the test, perhaps with a score, to help you become increasingly familiar with the characteristic sounds of these two important types of chromatic chord.

(a) (i) bar 8 (2); (ii) bar 28 (2); (iii) bar 16 (2). In each case allow (1) if there is a one-bar discrepancy.

(b) ½ + 11 × ½ (6)

(c) 12 × ½ (6)

(d) (i) diminished 7th (1); Ic (1); V⁷b (of G major) (1); augmented 6th (1). Note: for Paper 61 you won't be required to spot the differences between various types of augmented 6th chord (Italian, German, French). But consult *The Rhinegold Dictionary of Music in Sound* if you want to pursue the matter for your own interest and information. Note also that in these answers, chords other than the diminished 7th, augmented 6th and Neapolitan 6th are referred to by roman numerals (I, V, IVb, etc.). Where a chord is in the starting key of the test, no key is given. Where a chord can be described most accurately and/or simply in terms of a key other than the tonic, the answers will show this, e.g. 'V⁷b (of G major)'.

(ii) C major (1)

(iii) A minor (1)

(iv) appoggiatura (1)

(v) (modified) sequence (1)

(e) (i) texture: melody-dominated homophony (at start) (1), Alberti bass (at bar 9) (1); form: (first) part / exposition (1) from a binary / sonata form (1) movement, ending in A minor / dominant minor (1); harmony: chromatic harmonic language (1), with (numerous) diminished 7ths and/or augmented 6ths (1) and false relations (1), and dissonances include appoggiaturas (1); rhythm / melody: highly ornamented / florid / many short note values (1) with turns (1). Max. 8
As indicated at the top of page 50, if you offer correct and relevant information that is not listed here it could still receive credit (providing the points are not glaringly obvious from the score). Ask your teacher if in doubt.

(ii) piano sonata (1)

(iii) any year 1790–1827 (1). Beethoven (1). Informal / private recital *or* public concert (1)

Test 2

The music is the second movement from Handel's Concerto in F major, Op. 3, No. 4. Classified sometimes as a concerto grosso, sometimes as an oboe concerto, the work does not fall readily into any single category. The first movement is a purely orchestral French overture; the second has a part for oboe solo (although it is rarely independent of the first violins); the third employs two oboes, which largely double the violins. Handel's six concerti Op. 3 were published in London in 1734, although much of the music dates from well before this. Op. 3 No. 4, for example, was performed in 1716 at the King's Theatre, Haymarket, London as an 'orchestral concerto' between acts of the opera *Amadigi* – compare how the concerto you heard in Question 1, Test 3 (a), was played between the acts of an oratorio.

(a) (i) bar 47 (2); (ii) bar 52 (2); (iii) bar 41 (2). In each case allow (1) if there is a one-bar discrepancy.

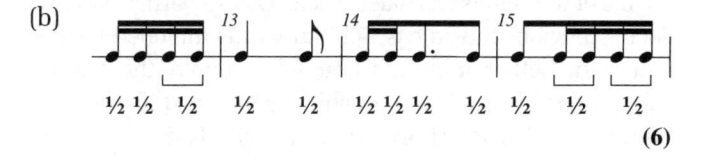

(b) (6)

(c) 12 × ½ (6)

(d) (i) IV (1); IIb (1); V⁷d (1)

(ii) imperfect (IVb V) / phrygian (1)

(iii) (7–6) suspension (1)

(iv) C major (1)

(v) B♭ (1); D minor (1)

(e) (i) instrumentation: oboe (and strings) (1); bassoon(s) (1); harpsichord (1); texture: melody-dominated homophony (1), (often with) parallel 3rds / 10ths (between outer parts) (1); harmony: diatonic (1), (largely with) primary triads and their inversions (1), inverted and/or dominant (1) pedal(s) (1); rhythm: some syncopation (1), hemiola (1); melodic style: (largely) conjunct (1) and triadic (1); (sometimes inexact) sequence (1); (oboe) improvisatory / cadenza-like in Adagio (1); structure: (brief) reprise of opening (at bar 28) (1) (not in fact ternary, nor easily classified according to 'standard' forms); based mainly on the opening four bars (almost suggesting ritornello) (1). Max. 8

(ii) concerto grosso / orchestral concerto / oboe concerto (1); moderately slow tempo (1); ending with imperfect or phrygian cadence / concluding with a 'link' passage / finishing with a modulation to a new key / or similar (1). Max. 2. The Adagio ending is very typical of Handel. Note the opportunity for soloistic improvisation and the strongly-emphasised phrygian cadence that leaves the movement 'open' ready for new music at a quicker tempo. Bach rarely used this kind of ending, but there is an example in the second movement of Brandenburg Concerto No. 4 (a work whose first movement appears in *The New Anthology of Music*).

(iii) any year 1680–1750 (1). Handel / Corelli / Albinoni / Vivaldi / other early 18th-century Italian or Italianate composer of concerti (1)

Test 3

This excerpt is the opening of the Agnus Dei, the penultimate item from Bach's B minor Mass. Bach completed this substantial work in the late 1740s, compiling and adapting much of it from his earlier compositions. The origins of the Agnus Dei date back to 1735 or earlier. Most of Bach's religious music has German words intended for the Protestant Lutheran church (see, for example, the cantata 'Ich elender Mensch', part of which is included in *The New Anthology of Music*). However, works with Latin texts were also sometimes performed in Lutheran services.

(a) (i) bar 15 (2); (ii) bar 22 (2); (iii) bar 13 (2). In each case allow (1) for a one-bar discrepancy.

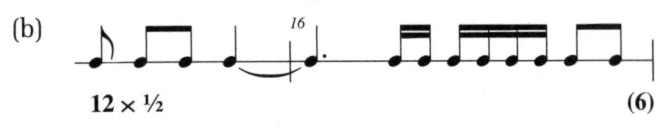

(b) [music notation] 12 × ½ (6)

(c) [music notation] 12 × ½ (6)

(d) (i) I (1); Neapolitan 6th (1)
    (ii) D minor (1)
    (iii) C minor (1)
    (iv) 7–6 (½) suspension (½)
    (v) V (1), Vb (1), I (1)

(e) (i) forces: contralto (1), <u>organ</u> continuo (1) with cello (1); rhythm: syncopation in <u>melody line(s)</u> (1), bass rests on weak quavers (1); melody: angular / disjunct (1), (some) chromatic(ism) (1) and sequence (1); harmony: (occasional) false relations (e.g. bar 11) (1); minor key <u>throughout</u> (1); texture: (initially) melody-dominated homophony / chordal accompaniment (1), <u>then</u> (1) (some) imitation (1) between voice and violin / accompaniment (1); structure: a clear reference to ritornello (1). Max. 8

(ii) Mass (1)

(iii) any year 1720–60 (1); J S Bach / Handel (1); (Lutheran) church / at Mass (1)

Test 4

Haydn's Quartet Op. 76 No. 2 was composed and published in the late 1790s. You can easily hear why it gained its nickname 'Fifths'! The work was probably intended for private rather than public concert performance. Notice the sometimes very high violin 1 part, and the far-reaching tonal scheme, with its shift to F minor (from F major) at bar 32, and then to A♭, the relative major of F minor – so that, quite logically, we have travelled as far from the opening D minor as it is possible to travel.

(a) (i) bar 41 (2); (ii) bar 23 (2); (iii) bar 13 (2). In each case allow (1) for a one-bar discrepancy.

(b) [music notation] 12 × ½ (6)

(c) [music notation] ½ ½ ½ ½ ½ ½ ½ ½ ½ ½ ½ ½ (6)

(d) (i) imperfect / phrygian (1)
    (ii) G minor (1)
    (iii) perfect (1)
    (iv) Ib (1); IIb (1); Ic (1); V^7 (1) / V (½), all in F major
    (v) F major (1)

(e) (i) no credit for identifying instruments; texture: varied (1): melody-dominated homophony (at start) (1); two-part and / or three-part (1); chordal (bar 25) (1); monophonic <u>at end</u> (1); form: (first) part / exposition (1) from a binary / sonata form (1) movement (no credit for ending in relative major / F major, in view of (d) (v)); harmony: functional (1) and largely diatonic (1); clear / located reference to chromatic movement (1), to F minor (1) and A♭ major (1); rhythm: clear / located reference to syncopation (1) and to reliance on repeated rhythmic patterns (1); melody: (quick) scalic movement (1) alternating with fifths (shown too frequently in the score for a mark to be awarded for these!) and triadic patterns (1). Max. 8

(ii) string quartet (1)

(iii) any year 1785–1807 (1); Haydn / Mozart (1); domestic / private music-making / private concert (1)

Test 5

This extract is the opening of the second movement of Beethoven's Symphony No. 4, Op. 60, completed in 1806 and first performed the following year. Although on a smaller scale than the preceding 'Eroica' Symphony, the work breaks new ground with its rapid Menuetto, which now has Beethoven's characteristic expanded double trio structure. It is also notable for its testing instrumental demands, notably the bassoon writing in the breakneck finale. The 'larger' orchestral sounds and textures of the second movement mark it out as being the work of Beethoven rather than Haydn or Mozart.

(a) (i) bar 28 (2); (ii) bar 35 (2) / bar 37 (1); (iii) bar 22 / 23 (2). In each case allow (1) if there is a one-bar discrepancy.

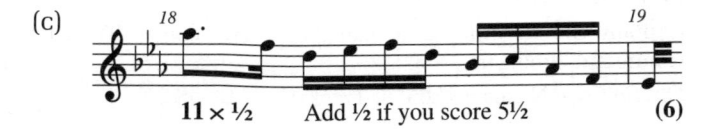

(b) 12 × ½ (6)

(c) 11 × ½   Add ½ if you score 5½ (6)

(d) (i) bar 19 (½), beat 3 (½)

(ii) C minor (1)

(iii) B♭ (1)

(iv) (7–6) suspension (1)

(v) diminished 7th (1); IIb (1); Ic (1); V^7 (1) / V (½), in B♭ major

(e) (i) instrumentation: standard (late) classical orchestra (1), including timpani (1), with pizzicato lower strings (1); texture: melody-dominated homophony (1), (reduced at some points to) two parts (1); form: on the basis of this excerpt, accept ternary (1) – a better alternative is: (first) part / exposition (1) from a binary / sonata form (1) movement; harmony: functional (1) and mainly diatonic (1); tonality: major (1) with modulation to the dominant (no mark: this is covered by (d) (iii)) with final return to the tonic (E♭) (1); rhythm: steady pulse with characteristic 'heartbeat' figure (1), triplets and/or demisemiquavers (1); melody: mainly conjunct (1) as in descending main theme (1). Max. 8

(ii) symphony (1)

(iii) any year 1795–1828 (1); Beethoven / Schubert (1); public concert (1)

Test 6

Test 6 is based on part of the first movement from Smetana's Piano Trio in G minor, Op. 15. The work was composed in the mid 1850s after the death of the composer's daughter. This circumstance is reflected in the anguished melodic lines and (for those times) extreme dissonance, notably a grinding succession of parallel augmented 4ths (tritones) from bar 34 – although some kind of peace seems to have been attained by the end of the excerpt.

(a) (i) bar 41 (2); (ii) bar 29 (1); (iii) bar 4 (2). In each case allow (1) if there is a one-bar discrepancy.

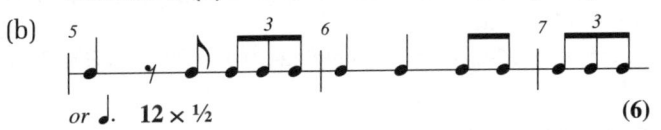

(b) or ♩. 12 × ½ (6)

(c) 12 × ½ (6)

(d) (i) diminished 7th (1) and false relation / appoggiatura (1)

(ii) B♭ (1)

(iii) Neapolitan 6th (1)

(iv) G major (1)

(v) V (1); VI (1); III (1), all in G major

(e) (i) instrumentation: violin, cello and piano / piano trio (1); texture: monophonic opening (1), (then violin with) broken chord accompaniment (1), piano chords with independent lines on strings (1); (then two-part) canon (1) between strings in octaves (1) and piano, producing a series of descending parallel tritones (1); harmony: extremely dissonant (1) with diminished 7th chords (1), augmented 6ths (1), pedal points (1) and false relation(s) (1); rhythm: some syncopation (1), dotted rhythms and/or triplets common (1); melodic lines angular (1), often chromatic (1), sometimes sequential (1). Max. 8

(ii) piano trio (1)

(iii) any year 1840–80 (1); Smetana / Dvořák / Brahms (1); public concert / private performance by highly accomplished performers (or similar) (1)

Track Information by Question

Question 1

Test 1 (a): Track 1
Purcell: *Scorned Envy* (from Act III of *The Indian Queen*)
Scholars Baroque Ensemble, Robin Doveton (tenor)
Naxos 8.553752, Track 15, 0:00–0:59

Test 1 (b): Track 2
Beethoven: String Quartet in F minor, Op. 95, Movement III
Kodály Quartet
Naxos 8.554181, Track 7, 0:00–0:48

Test 1 (c): Track 3
Tavener: *The Tiger*
Choir of St John's College, Cambridge, Christopher Robinson (cond)
Naxos 8.555256, Track 4, 4:30–5:20

Test 2 (a): Track 4
J S Bach: *St John Passion* ('Simon Petrus' and 'Ich folge dir')
Scholars Baroque Ensemble, Robin Doveton (tenor), Janet Coxwell (soprano)
Naxos 8.550664, Track 8 complete, 0:00–0:15 and Track 9, 0:00–0:38

Test 2 (b): Track 5
Stravinsky: *I Was Never Saner* (from *The Rake's Progress*)
Münchner Rundfunk Orchester, Samuel Ramey (bass), Julius Rudel (cond)
A Date with the Devil Naxos 8.555355, Track 12, 1:12–2:10

Test 2 (c): Track 6
Dizzy Gillespie/Frank Paparelli: *A Night in Tunisia*
Dizzy Gillespie (trumpet), Charlie Parker (alto saxophone), John Lewis (piano), Al McKibbon (bass), Joe Harris (drums)
Charlie: Bird on the Side Naxos 8.120622, Track 17, 0:00–0:50

Test 3 (a): Track 7
Handel: Concerto Grosso in C major (Allegro from *Alexander's Feast*)
Capella Istropolitana, Jozef Kopelman (cond)
Naxos 8.550158, Track 18, 0:00–0:42

Test 3 (b): Track 8
Puccini: *Vissi d'arte, vissi d'amore* (from Act II of *Tosca*)
Slovak Philharmonic Chorus, Czecho-Slovak Radio Symphony Orchestra (Bratislava), Alexander Rahbari (cond), Nelly Miricioiu (soprano)
Naxos 8.660002, Track 12, 2:17–3:18

Test 3 (c): Track 9
Bessie Smith: *Jail House Blues*
Bessie Smith (vocals), Irving Johns (piano)
Bessie: Downhearted Blues Naxos 8.120660, Track 10, 0:00–1:00

Test 4 (a): Track 10
Monteverdi: *Vespers* ('Sicut erat' from the Magnificat)
Scholars Baroque Ensemble
Naxos 8.550663, Track 14, 0:55–1:46

Liszt: Preludio in C major
Jenö Jandó (piano)
Etudes d'exécution transcendante Naxos 8.553119, Track 1, complete 0:00–0:54

Test 4 (c): Track 12
Rory Gallagher: *Shin kicker*
Etched in Blue BMG 74321 627972, Track 14, 0:00–1:26

Test 5 (a): Track 13
Byrd: *Pavan*
Rose Consort of Viols, Red Byrd
The Glory of Early Music Naxos 8.554064, Track 17, 0:00–0:33

Test 5 (b): Track 14
Dolly Parton: *Coat of many colors*
Ultimate Dolly Parton BMG 82876 54201 2, Track 6, 0:00–0:53

Test 5 (c): Track 15
Ravel: *La Vallée des cloches*
François-Joël Thiollier (piano)
Piano Works Naxos 8.550683, Track 17, 0:00–0:48

Test 6 (a): Track 16
Orlande de Lassus: *Lauda mater ecclesia*
Oxford Camerata, Jeremy Summerly (cond)
Renaissance Masterpieces Naxos 8.550843, Track 8, 0:00–1:07

Test 6 (b): Track 17
Schoenberg: *Drei Klavierstücke*, Op. 11, No. 3
Peter Hill (piano)
Naxos 8.553870, Track 4, 0:00–0:43

Test 6 (c): Track 18
Carmichael-Parish: *Stardust*
Captain Glenn Miller and The Army Air Forces Training Command Orchestra
Oh, So Good Naxos 8.120573, Track 17, 0:13–0:59

Test 7 (a): Track 19
Elgar: *Imperial March*, Op. 32
BBC Philharmonic, George Hurst (cond)
Naxos 8.550634, Track 1, 0:00–1:09

Test 7 (b): Track 20
Schoenberg: *Suite*, Op. 25 (Trio)
Peter Hill (piano)
Naxos 8.553870, Track 22 complete, 0:00–0:39

Test 7 (c): Track 21
Neil Sedaka: *Happy Birthday, Sweet Sixteen*
The Best of Neil Sedaka BMG PA 777/2, Track 13, 0:00–1:03

Test 8 (a): Track 22
J S Bach: *Wir Christenleut*
Wolfgang Rübsam (organ)
Naxos 8.553135, Track 12, 0:00–0:57

Test 8 (b): Track 23
Haydn: Symphony No. 8 in G major ('Le Soir')
Northern Chamber Orchestra, Nicholas Ward (cond)
Naxos 8.550722, Track 9, 0:00–1:02

Test 8 (c): Track 24
Monk: *Epistrophy*
Thelonious Monk Quartet
Monk's Moods Naxos 8.120588, Track 16, 0:19–1:03

Question 2

Test 1 (a): Track 25
Elgar: Symphony No. 1, Movement I
BBC Philharmonic, George Hurst (cond)
Naxos 8.550634, Track 2, 0:00–3:17

Test 1 (b): Track 26
Elgar: Symphony No. 1, Movement IV
BBC Philharmonic, George Hurst (cond)
Naxos 8.550634, Track 5, 8:36–end

Test 2 (a): Track 27
Sibelius: Symphony No. 5 (Finale)
Iceland Symphony Orchestra, Petri Sakari (cond)
Naxos 8.554377, Track 7, 0:50–2:30

Test 2 (b): Track 28
Sibelius: Symphony No. 5 (Finale)
Iceland Symphony Orchestra, Petri Sakari (cond)
Naxos 8.554377, Track 7, 3:51–6:32

Test 3 (a): Track 29
Beethoven: Triple Concerto, Movement I
Dong-Suk Kang (violin), Maria Kliegel (cello), Jenö Jandó (piano), Nicolaus Esterhazy Sinfonia, Béla Drahos (cond)
Naxos 8.554288, Track 4, 0:00–1:09

Test 3 (b): Track 30
Beethoven: Triple Concerto, Movement I
Dong-Suk Kang (violin), Maria Kliegel (cello), Jenö Jandó (piano), Nicolaus Esterhazy Sinfonia, Béla Drahos (cond)
Naxos 8.554288, Track 4, 2:27–3:53

Test 4 (a): Track 31
Monteverdi: *Vespers* (Magnificat)
Scholars Baroque Ensemble
Naxos 8.550663, Track 9, 0:00–2:31

Test 4 (b): Track 32
Monteverdi: *Vespers* (Magnificat)
Scholars Baroque Ensemble
Naxos 8.550663, Track 11, 0:00–1:19

Test 5 (a): Track 33
Mahler: Symphony No. 3, Movement I
Polish National Radio Symphony Orchestra, Antoni Wit (cond)
Naxos 8.550525, Track 1, 6:44–8:50

Test 5 (b): Track 34
Mahler: Symphony No. 7, Movement I
Polish National Radio Symphony Orchestra, Michael Halasz
Naxos 8.550531, Track 1, 0:00–2:16

Test 6 (a): Track 35
Britten: *War Requiem* (Offertorium)
Scottish Festival Chorus, BBC Scottish Symphony Orchestra, Martyn Brabbins (cond)
Naxos 8.553559, Track 3, 1:19–3:21

Test 6 (b): Track 36
Britten: *War Requiem* (Offertorium)
Scottish Festival Chorus, BBC Scottish Symphony Orchestra, Martyn Brabbins (cond)
Naxos 8.553559, Track 3, 8:20–end

Question 3

Test 1: Tracks 37–39
Beethoven: Piano Sonata, Op. 10, No. 3, Movement II
Jenö Jandó (piano)
Naxos 8.550161, Track 8, 0:00–3:08

Test 2: Tracks 40–43
Handel: Concerto Op. 3 No. 4, Movement II
Northern Sinfonia, Bradley Creswick (director)
Naxos 8.553457, Track 14 complete, 0:00–2:08

Test 3: Tracks 44–47
Bach: B minor Mass (Agnus Dei)
Martina Koppelstetter (alto), Capella Istropolitana, Christian Brembeck (cond)
Naxos 8.550586, Track 14, 0:00–3:54

Test 4: Tracks 48–51
Haydn: Quartet in D minor, Op. 76, No. 2, Movement I
Kodály Quartet
Naxos 8.550129, Track 5, 0:00–1:46

Test 5: Tracks 52–55
Beethoven: Symphony No. 4. Movement II
Zagreb Philharmonic, Richard Edlinger (cond)
Naxos 8.550180, Track 6, 0:00–3:35

Test 6: Tracks 56–59
Smetana: Trio in G minor, Movement I
Joachim Trio
Naxos 8.553415, Track 1, 7:25–9:27